lilac ROOTS

ONE WOMAN'S STORY OF
FINDING PEACE IN THE STORM

BRENDA FITZMAURICE

© 2018 Brenda Fitzmaurice
Published by Lilac Roots, LLC
Merrill, Michigan

Printed in the United States of America

All rights reserved

Scriptures taken from the Holy Bible, New International Version®, NIV®. Copyright © 1973, 1978, 1984, 2011 by Biblica, Inc.™ Used by permission of Zondervan. All rights reserved worldwide. www.zondervan.com The "NIV" and "New International Version" are trademarks registered in the United States Patent and Trademark Office by Biblica, Inc.™

ISBN-13: 978-1729584866
ISBN-10: 1729584861

Dad,
You are missed.
You are loved.
You are thought of often.

DEDICATION

To my family who have been through so much more than anything we could have imagined.

To my mom for being stronger than you are given credit for and for always being there when I get in a bind or when I want your ear to share exciting news. I know you are always equally excited for me.

To my husband who has put up with my ups and downs and stuck through it. You have been my "Jack of all trades", a good husband, partner and father. Thank you for helping with our girls and household chores more often to free up my time to write this book.

To my Facebook support group for all your positive comments, prayers and encouragement as I undertook this writing journey of mine.

contents

FOREWORD 1
INTRODUCTION 3

CHAPTER 1
FAMILY 5

CHAPTER 2
ROOTS 23

CHAPTER 3
BROKEN 33

CHAPTER 4
BRANCHING OUT 53

CHAPTER 5
DARKNESS 59

CHAPTER 6
BATTERED BY THE STORM 71

CHAPTER 7
GROWTH 83

CHAPTER 8
LOVE 93

CHAPTER 9
HOME 103

CHAPTER 10
FINDING ANSWERS 121

CHAPTER 11
SEASONS 131

CHAPTER 12
FLOURISH 141

HELP WHILE YOU'RE IN THE STORM 149
ABOUT THE AUTHOR 157
NOTES 159

FOREWORD

In this tech-centric age where people are able to hide behind keyboards and divvy out epic unkindness – or publish only their life's highlight reel - it's easier than ever to feel alone in our own messy, unglamorous lives. But sometimes the grass is greener on the other side...because it's fake. Everyone has a story, and most people are fighting battles we'll never know anything about. Pain is inevitable in this beautiful and broken world. Whether you're a princess or a paraplegic, you will feel the ache; for our condition is the *human* condition.

While we don't get to opt out of pain, we do get to choose what we'll do with it; whether we will allow it to make us bitter, or make us better. We can stay stuck and alone in the ache, or we can bring the broken pieces to our Maker who somehow manages to create beauty from our pain.

> "I have made you. I will carry you;
> I will sustain you and I will rescue you."
>
> *Isaiah 46:4*

The sting of rejection is one that lingers. Add tremendous loss to the mix - and all the unanswered questions that accompany it - and you're left with a deep sorrow that burrows its way into the soul, slowly poisoning the way you see everything. It's a joy-stealer and hope-killer if left to fester.

I've had the privilege of walking closely with Brenda as she's wrestled with her story this past year, emerging stronger and wiser. A force to be reckoned with. Sweeter still, is her willingness to extend her journey to others, inviting them not only into her pain, but into her healing and freedom.

May your heart be encouraged by her journey, and may peace and freedom be yours. Indeed, God wastes nothing.

Joy McMillan

INTRODUCTION

I have a story I would like to tell. It's a difficult story to tell, but I feel it's necessary to share it. It's my story and nobody else's, although there may be similarities with those of others. It's a sad story but, at the same time, it's a hopeful one.

My story is about bullying and suicide and finding peace in the midst of a storm.

I want children, teenagers and adults who have been the victims of bullying, or who are themselves the perpetrator of bullying, to hear my story. I want those who have ever contemplated suicide to know how loved they truly are, to understand the devastation that suicide causes to those left behind, and to ultimately experience the hope that I have. That is my mission.

Nobody has a perfect life. Almost everyone we encounter has had to overcome death of a loved one. And everyone has struggles in their life at one point or another. None of us are immune to hardship and heartache.

And yet, I believe that no matter what obstacles life throws at us, it will work out. I have come to believe that God has a plan and a purpose for our lives. Learning to discover this purpose, to find moments of happiness in between the pain and to discover the strength and ability we have to grow through the storms, is what makes all of it worthwhile.

This book is not for educational purposes. This is my life story. These are my thoughts, feelings and opinions on bullying and suicide. Through baring my soul, and opening up about my painful experiences, as well as the redemptive perspective I now have on these moments, my wish is that you will know that I survived and you will too, no matter what you are dealing with today.

My story has not been an easy one, but sharing it in this way has brought healing, hope and a measure of wholeness I couldn't have imagined. I trust that it will do the same for you.

Some names and identifying details in this book have been changed to protect the privacy of individuals.

CHAPTER 1
family

Fam·i·ly
fam(ə)lē

Noun 1. a group consisting of parents and children living together in a household. 2. all the descendants of a common ancestor.
Synonyms: clan, people, kinfolk, relations, relatives
'The house has been owned by the same family for 300 years."

I was your typical, active girl. I loved riding my bike back and forth to my grandparents' house, jumping rope, shopping, decorating and moving furniture around in my bedroom. I loved make-up of all shades, and fixing my sister's hair ... or anyone who would let me! My favorite color was pink.

I had a "tomboy" side though. Maybe this was a result of growing up on a farm? I liked to go fishing with my older brother, Patrick, rough riding through the woods, sledding behind our Big Red Honda 250 three-wheeler, and playing in the hay mow. We would align and stack bales of hay to make walls and build a house. In the mow, we would create a "pretend" house with a kitchen, living room, bathroom and bedroom. We'd also pile up loose straw on the main level of the barn and jump in it from the mow. We had so much fun spending many hours in that big red barn. Of course, after jumping in the straw, we'd have to pick it out of our pockets, shirt and pants before our mother would let us go back in the house!

I also enjoyed playing in our sand box that was made from

an old tractor tire. I would sit on the edge with my feet in the dirt and push my brother's matchbox cars and trucks around in the sand, or just build castles and mounds. I would have to watch out for the little surprises the barn cats would leave behind in the sand though!

But most of all I loved to climb up and hide in the large lilac bush in our yard. It grew so tall that it was actually more like a tree. I think it got so big because nobody pruned it, which it probably should have been. It gave me a hiding spot to spy on the cars coming in and out of our driveway. While perched in the bush, I would suck the sweetness out of the tiny lilac petals as I pulled them off their green stems. It was like sucking sugar from a straw. Oh how I loved the smell and look of the lilac blossoms when they were in full bloom! Sadly it only lasted for about three weeks of the year. During that short period, I would pick a large bouquet of flowers from the bush, put it in a clear vase of water and place it on the wooden desk next to my bed. As I walked up the thirteen steps to my bedroom, the smell would get stronger. To this day, every time I smell lilacs, I think of my childhood on that farm.

Lilacs have a variety of meanings throughout different cultures and time periods. Traditionally, the flower symbolizes a first love and confidence. In the United States, the lilac is the state flower of New Hampshire and represents the hardy nature of its people. In Russia, the flower is supposed to bring wisdom to a newborn while holding it over the infant. George Washington and Thomas Jefferson had an attraction for lilacs and grew them in their gardens. Lilacs represent a happy time on the farm for me. A time of opening our windows and letting in the fresh, wonderful, clean smell of the outdoors. They show that summer is upon us, a time to enjoy being outside after being huddled indoors throughout the dreary winter months.

I was soft spoken and short for my age, much like my grandma. I was born with black hair and little itty bitty blue eyes. My mom once told me the story about how, when she took me to my first doctor's appointment, the doctor asked her, "Which foreign family in the area are you babysitting for?" He probably questioned her because she has blond hair and big eyes and I was quite the opposite! My parents, along with my brother and sister, often laughed about what the doctor asked. My siblings would tease me and tell me that I was adopted, and that our mom and dad didn't love me as much as they loved them. Being somewhat naïve and sensitive, this would make me sad and I would cry thinking that my parents didn't love me as much as my siblings. My mom would reassure me that I looked just like my dad and his sister, and that I wasn't adopted. My dad also had small, bright blue eyes and dark hair. His eyes would appear even bluer when he'd wear his royal blue sweatshirt in the winter months. As I got a little older, my hair got a little lighter but never blonde like my mom's. When I reached the adolescent years, it got darker again. It's strange how that happens.

I'm not sure how my dad came up with my name but he was the one who named me. Maybe he got my first name from the country singer, Brenda Lee, since he loved country music? If I were a boy, my mom wanted to name me Maxwell (probably Max for short) but she couldn't think of a girl's name. So, Brenda Jane it was. Jane is after my mom and grandma's middle name. I was a surprise to my parents when my mom found out she was pregnant with me. I was delivered 2 years 5 months after my brother. My mom wanted many kids but she wanted to have us a little farther apart in age!

I am the youngest of three. Even though my sister, Connie, and I weren't close in age (there are 7 years between us), she and I still had fun playing together. We loved to play "school" and would use aged math books my parents had around the house. We would use an old large chalkboard which my mom probably found at a garage sale. We would construct our math problems on the board so we weren't writing in the books. I believe even at a young age my sister knew she wanted to be a teacher. She was really good at teaching me math and helping me with my homework when I would struggle with numbers. We would also play with Barbies and baby dolls together. I think almost every little girl I knew wanted to be a mom someday. There was something about holding that little doll and cuddling it that felt so wonderful. There was one particular doll that both my sister and I loved to play with. We named her Sara. Often she would only play dolls with me if I let her play with Sara. I'm a push-over, so I'd cave in. I really just wanted someone to play with me. It didn't bother me that I had to play with another doll. I'm not very outspoken or aggressive. I think I got trait from my dad.

My mom told me that I always felt I had to have someone to play with me when I was a toddler. My sister and brother would be at school and she would look around our six bedroom farmhouse for me and eventually find that I climbed in my crib and was taking a nap. I must've just been bored. I particularly didn't like it when Patrick started kindergarten. He and I seemed to play together more often than my sister and me. Maybe it's because we were closer in age? We would spend many hours playing together outside and I looked up to him. He was well liked by his peers in school and his good manners were raved about by the adults in our little community. He was a confident, blue eyed, sandy blonde-haired boy.

We were the average family ... if there really is such a thing. Saturday nights were spent watching *Hee Haw*, *Knight Rider* and *Different Strokes*. My dad also loved to watch the *Golden Girls*. He would get a lot of laughs out of Betty White. As I watch the reruns of that show, I don't think I really got the humor as a kid but I do now. My mom was a night owl and loved staying up late to enjoy *Johnny Carson*. My dad would make popcorn in the cast iron pan on the stove. It always seemed to turn out perfectly. He loved popcorn! Whenever we went somewhere that offered popcorn, he'd get a bag of it. Sometimes we would get Vernors (a brand of ginger ale) or 7up to drink on our Saturday evenings together but it wasn't very often that my mom would buy pop for us. We usually only had milk, orange juice or water in the house to drink and sometimes Kool-Aid in the summer.

I recall my dad playing a practical joke on my sister one Saturday evening after making his popcorn. Connie was in her teens but still wetting the bed. Looking back, I now know that there was a medical issue, however she did like to drink a lot before bed and this didn't help matters. On this particular evening, she wanted a second glass of Vernors Ginger Ale before going to bed. The Vernors was finished though so, without her noticing, my dad put approximately half a cup of vegetable oil in the Vernors bottle. My dad told her that she could have more to drink but that she'd better not wet the bed that night. My sister quickly drank what was left in the bottle. She drank almost all of it and wasn't coming up for air while drinking. Apparently she was drinking so fast that she wasn't tasting it either! Not until we were laughing, did she notice her lips were a little greasy. Luckily she saw the funny side of it too and we still laugh about it today!

My dad enjoyed playing little jokes like that on us. Sometimes he would intentionally initiate a conflict between my siblings and me, then walk away and laugh. My brother and I would be playing a board game, like Monopoly, and my dad would tell one of us that the other was cheating. Then he'd giggle and we knew he was just fibbing. On another occasion, we were all watching a scary movie in our living room and he reached down and pulled the cord out of the outlet on the floor lamp during a scary part. We screamed when the lights went out. Of course he laughed.

I can also vividly remember how he hid an Easter egg outside in a little hole in the yard. The Easter bunny always hid our eggs inside the house, and my dad knew that I'd walk past the hole on my way to my grandparents' house that Easter afternoon. I immediately noticed the egg and was so shocked that the Easter bunny had dropped it there. We thought we'd found all the eggs he left for us in the house! When I got to Grandma and Grandpa's house, I excitedly told them about it. My dad was grinning from ear to ear.

We would tease my dad often too. We called him "Baldy" due to the lack of hair on his head, which he would try to hide by doing a comb over to cover the bald spot. We'd also tease him about always wearing plaid button-down shirts. As I got older, I'd go shopping with my mom and pick out some plain or striped polo shirts for him, which at least he wore once or twice when we'd go out and about together.

My dad really enjoyed Christmas. He would cut down a tree at a local tree farm about a week before Christmas. It was usually a blue spruce because he liked the look of them. He would drag the large tree into our house and set it up using an old white metal tree stand. Every year, my mom would complain because he picked out such a full, fat tree that would take up the entire corner of the living room. It was a corner where people driving by could see the bright beautiful lights. The tree that my dad brought home would never be perfectly shaped. He would creatively cut branches and use shoe string or twine to lift any droopy branches to fill the gaps and achieve the perfect shape. By the time he was done, the tree looked so perfect that guests would think it was fake. He would then string the multi-colored lights around the tree and wrap the red, silver, gold and blue garland from top to bottom. Meanwhile, my siblings and I would wait patiently to start decorating with the ornaments. We would excitedly start placing the red, blue, gold and silver round, glass ornaments on along with any homemade decorations we made at school. Dad would place the Christmas tree topper on along with the ornaments towards the top of the tree where we couldn't reach. After all of the ornaments were on, we would then put the silver tinsel, piece by piece, all over the tree. My dad loved lots of tinsel! When the tree was complete, we would sit back and admire how beautiful it was. The natural pine smell was wonderful and permeated the entire house. It's amazing how the smell of a house can make it even cozier.

After trimming the tree one year, I got out the old paperback books of Christmas songs that were packed away with the boxes of Christmas decorations every year. My dad and I sat on the couch together and started singing. Mainly just to annoy my mom and brother. We couldn't hold a note to save our lives but we had such fun! We giggled while we sang. My favorite song was always *Away in a Manger*.

In the days leading up to Christmas, my brother and I would sit on his bed and look through the Sears Wish Book. We would look at every toy on each page and point to the items we would love to have. Every year we would talk about having the remote control airplane that was always pictured. We knew it was too expensive to ask for it, but we could always wish.

My dad was a farmer and a mailman, but his real passion was farming. As I look back, I don't know where he got the energy he had. He would get up automatically (without an alarm clock) at 5:30 every morning and go out to the barn, sometimes in extremely cold weather. He would feed the cows, pigs and chickens, gather the eggs and then get ready to go on his mail route. He'd go to the post office by 8 a.m., sort the mail and then drive many miles on the country roads delivering mail until 3 p.m. Then back in the barn he'd go to feed the animals and either start planting crops in the field if it was spring or, if it was autumn, he'd be harvesting. He would be out in the fields after dark on many days in the fall to harvest sugar beets. Then back up in the morning for the routine to start again. I think having that kind of passion gave him the energy he needed to succeed.

I also believe he got the energy and motivation from his desire to provide for his family. He wanted to give us a good life and show us that you have to work for what you get. I think that is how he showed his love for us. My dad wasn't very affectionate towards us kids, we would sit on his lap sometimes but I don't recall him tucking me in or giving me a kiss good night or saying "I love you". He showed his love by providing for us and we accepted that.

Growing up on a farm taught me many things that have helped me in my life today. It taught me good work ethics, to not take things for granted and that not everything will be handed to you on a silver platter; it taught me to actually enjoy the outdoors and nature; and it showed me how awesome God is to have created the ground and dirt to grow plants to be able to put food on the table. It is hard work to plant and grow your own garden! Every summer from third grade onwards, I helped hoe weeds out of the bean fields. We walked many acres and did this all of July and into August. However, as a kid, all I wanted to do was sleep in everyday and play during my summer break.

We would get up around 6:30 a.m., eat a quick breakfast, usually a bowl of cold cereal, and leave for the bean field around 7 a.m. We would be out there until noon and then drive back home in my dad's 1972 yellow and white pickup truck with the kids (myself, my brother and sister, along with my cousins) riding in the back. On a hot summer day, this would feel really good with my hair blowing in the wind. My mom would have dinner ready for us at exactly 12 o'clock. We called it dinner, although some people call it lunch - in parts of the US, supper and dinner are used interchangeably to refer to the evening meal, but elsewhere dinner is the midday meal or the main meal of the day. Then at 1 p.m. we'd go back out to the fields to work until 6 p.m. It was a long day, especially if it was 85 degrees with 90% humidity! My mom would then have supper on the table for us. Once in a while my grandparents would take all of us kids to McDonald's for supper after hoeing. This was a big treat for us. The closest McDonald's was about 20 miles away.

My mom, Charlotte, is the younger of two children. She has an older brother, Bobby. She grew up in a tiny house with concrete block walls in Omer, Michigan. She shared a bedroom with her parents while her brother's bedroom was the living room. She was a nervous, shy, skinny girl with blonde hair and blue eyes. She has always been a very giving and loving person, but lacked self-confidence. She was a hard worker but barely passed high school. School studies did not come easily to her. She didn't get the support from her parents who weren't highly educated. Her dad worked on the county's road commission and her mom was a homemaker. Her dad was an alcoholic, which would trigger her mom's bad temper when he'd come home drunk. My mom witnessed many occasions in which her mom would slap her dad out of anger over his drinking. Her dad was mellow though, and he thankfully never hit her back. My grandmother would prepare a nice supper and he would not eat much after filling up on beer at the local bar on his way home from work. A few times, she got so upset that she tipped over the supper table and my mom had to clean up the glass and the mess while crying and asking them to stop fighting. My mom did not want this life when she got older and did not want it for her children.

Unfortunately, my mom's parents passed away at an early age. Her dad passed away from a heart attack 3 months after I was born and her mom passed away from cancer when I was 5 years old. I do recall the few fun times I had with my grandma. She stayed with us while she was sick and she used to play board games with me. I have a memory of her burping a lot ... that must've been the nasty cancer getting to her! The cancer spread through her body quickly and once it got to her liver, she couldn't fight it anymore.

My mom was a stay-at-home mom who made sure the house was clean, laundry done, and dinner and supper on the table at noon and 6 p.m. precisely. She was the one who drove us the 5 miles to and from school for any extra activities we had. When I became a teenager, she became a nurse's aide and worked in a local nursing home. She was still able to do all of her motherly duties and had time to go shopping whenever I got the urge. My mom is the most giving and sincere person anyone could meet. She has always been a giver and a people pleaser.

Often on a Saturday my mom and I would leave our house at around 9 or 10 a.m., drive 1 hour to the nearest large city to go to the mall, and shop all day. We would scour the mall all afternoon to see if any articles of clothing caught our eye that we just couldn't live without. Many times though we were just window shopping, walking around, "people watching", eating freshly baked pretzels and enjoying a Coke. Then we'd head to Target to do more shopping and stop at a favorite restaurant and have a nice meal around 8 p.m. That was our bonding time. We would sit in a booth in the restaurant and chat about anything and everything. After getting our bellies full, we'd hit Meijer, the large grocery store that had everything from groceries to housewares to clothing. Meijer was open 24 hours so we could shop as long as we liked. After being gone for almost 12 hours, we'd head home. Of course, it would usually take us longer getting home because it would now be dark, so we'd have to drive slower to be cautious of deer jumping in front of us on our country roads. I loved those Saturdays with my mom!

My mom has a cousin, Marsha, who is almost like a sister to her and an aunt to me. They hung out as kids quite often and Marsha even lived with my parents for a short period of time before I was born. My mom and I could confide in Marsha and tell or ask her anything. Whenever I needed an adult opinion regarding boys or anything that I couldn't talk to my mom about, I'd ask Marsha. I really looked up to her. She was stylish, a lot of fun and easy to talk to. We are still close to her.

Not many children have the privilege of living within walking distance of their grandparents' house as we did. I loved walking through the large garden which was approximately 30 feet wide by 60 feet long to go and see Grandma and Grandpa, my father's parents. As a 9 or 10 year old, I would walk there after supper and Grandma would help me learn my spelling words, and then she'd usually give me a flashlight to walk back home with. I don't know how, but my grandma had a way of teaching me my spelling words very quickly. She would have been a wonderful teacher but she was a farmer's wife for all the many years that she was married to my grandpa.

My grandma was a hard worker. She helped plant the large garden that would provide food for herself and my grandpa, for my whole family, and sometimes for my dad's brother and his family too. There were many rows of corn, cabbage, potatoes, radishes, raspberries, carrots, green beans and tomatoes. My mom and grandma would can tomatoes yearly and freeze corn. We were well provided for by the canned goods all year. They would also can pears, peaches and applesauce. We had our own beef from the cows and pork from the pigs, meat and eggs from the chickens. We really did live mostly off our land. It was hard work but well worth it and healthier than the processed foods found in the stores.

My grandma was quiet and a very private person who

always cared what other people thought about her. She did not want to stand out or seem unusual. She was not flashy and did not drive expensive vehicles or wear expensive clothes. She was always concerned about what other people might think about how they lived. She did not talk about her childhood or her roots either. Unfortunately, I didn't learn much about her because I didn't ask many questions and she didn't voluntarily share her story. I regret this now, I wish I'd taken time to talk to her more.

My grandpa was also a hard worker. That's probably where my dad got most of his skills and work ethic from. My grandpa's parents came to Michigan from Northern Europe, from an area which was then called Prussia. Prussia covered large parts of what is now Germany, and also included areas of Poland. My grandpa had three brothers, one of them being his identical twin, and four sisters. Some might have said that he was what one would jokingly call a "typical German" - very structured and he always thought he was right! This would drive my grandma and my dad crazy! If you were to ask my husband, he'd probably say I was 100% German due to the fact that I like to think I'm always right!

My grandpa was very affectionate though. He would grab hold of me when I was younger and slap a slobbery kiss on my cheek. He would also tease me about this and that. That's probably where my dad got his sense of humor.

My dad worried a lot, mostly about the weather and whether there would be enough rain or too much rain for his crops. My grandpa on the other hand would just say, "We have to take what the good Lord gives us." My grandparents were very humble people. They did not live above their means and my dad chose to live the same way. New cars were a rarity and we got mostly used furnishings in our home. I remember we were one of the last among my friends to get a VCR and the luxury of a microwave. My dad and grandpa had to save their money for the farm. New tractors, combines, fertilizer and seed came first.

For many years my dad helped my grandpa in his fields until he earned enough money and bought his own acreage to farm. Just before I was born, my parents moved from their three bedroom trailer house my dad bought when they got married, into our six bedroom, one bathroom farmhouse. This farmhouse was where my dad and his two siblings grew up. My grandparents then had a two bedroom ranch style house built next to ours.

I always felt full of pride to show people where I lived. It showed that I came from a family of hard workers. Our big white farmhouse stood out from most homes. We had many outbuildings including a detached car garage; a large red shed that housed our tractors, trucks and combines; a red barn and silo; a gray outbuilding for our chickens; a little shack for our pigs and a white doghouse for Chip, our German shepherd mix.

My dad's younger brother, Ron, went to college and became a school teacher and married the girl he met in college. They only lived about 7 miles down the road from us along with their three boys. My dad's sister, with her husband and three children, lived in Bay City, about an hour from our farm.

We were a very close family. Every holiday we would get together either at our farmhouse or my grandparents' house for dinner. It was tradition that every Christmas Eve, we would go to church, the kids would perform a Christmas program with singing and verse readings for the adults and then we would go back to my grandparents' house. There we would eat the goodies my grandma had baked for us - homemade cookies, Rice Krispy treats and chocolate peanut clusters. Yummy! Then we would unwrap the gifts we received from our aunts and uncles. At around 11 p.m., we would watch the news on TV to track where Santa was in his sleigh. It was amazing as a child to see Santa on TV in his sleigh traveling the world! On Christmas Day, we would get together with the same family members for dinner and my cousins and I would share and talk about what we got from Santa and play with our new toys. Sometimes my mom's brother and his family would join us too.

Looking back now, my early childhood and upbringing seem almost idyllic. Fresh air, open fields, sunshine and home-grown food. But it was my family, the people who surrounded me and loved me, who gave me my roots. As symbolized by the beautiful lilac flowers I enjoyed so much, I grew in confidence and gained resilience. Years later, I would need these characteristics more than I would ever have dreamed possible.

> *"Call it a clan, call it a network, call it a tribe,*
> *call it a family: Whatever you call it,*
> *whoever you are, you need one."*
> *Jane Howard*

Me as a baby & little girl

Connie & me at Christmas time

Dad & mom

Grandma cooking Christmas dinner 1987

Grandpa resting in our recliner/rocking chair

CHAPTER 2

roots

Root
root

Noun 1. *the part of a plant which attaches it to the ground or to a support, typically underground, conveying water and nourishment to the rest of the plant via numerous branches and fibers.*
2. *the basic cause, source, or origin of something*
Synonyms: *origin, cause, core, essence, foundation*
"*money is the root of all evil*"
Verb 1. *to establish deeply and firmly.*
"*I was rooted in my seat while she spoke*"

Learning about someone's background or roots has always been interesting to me. It can often explain a lot about a person, such as why they have a certain way of talking, the words they use or why they act the way they do, or even just why they do what they do.

    I wasn't a latchkey kid, I never felt unloved or neglected. I lived with both of my parents and saw my grandparents often. I wasn't lazy either – I never sat around watching TV all day. I was, one would say, a normal kid growing up in the 70's and 80's. In our home, we sat around the supper table in the evening and talked about our day. Sometimes my parents would ask us questions like, "What grades did you get today?" Or my dad would be goofy and ask, "What boy kissed you today?"

    I think growing up in a small community sometimes sheltered me. It made me oblivious to what this world could be like. Not every child had both parents under one roof, and not every child lived next to and saw their grandparents on almost a daily basis. I've realized that it's easy to take the seemingly small stuff for granted and not show your appreciation. My family wasn't perfect by any means. My siblings and I would fight and have disagreements, we didn't always agree with the rules my parents had for us and my parents still had spats like every normal married couple do.

Although my parents didn't argue very often, when they did argue it was mostly about the way in which my grandparents interfered in my parents' business and encroached on their personal space. It reminds me of the TV show *Everybody Loves Raymond* where Ray's parents constantly show up at any time of the day and want to know what's going on, voicing their opinions on a matter even if they weren't asked. Having my grandparents living so close by was an advantage in so many ways, and as children we benefited much from it, but it meant that my parents did not have the privacy they should have had. My mom had a hard time living next to her in-laws and living in the house that was theirs for so many years.

When she married my dad, I think my mom felt very blessed. She married the only man she had ever fallen in love with. I think she believed that it was the start of only good things for her. No more worrying about money. She had a cozy home to take care of, and she now belonged to my dad's tight-knit family. But when they moved into my grandparents' farmhouse she realized that the life she thought she had wasn't actually hers. It was my dad's, my grandpa's and my grandma's. The large spacious home never felt like it actually belonged to her. Whenever my mom wanted new furniture to replace the old furniture which my grandparents left behind, or when she wanted to do something as simple as painting a room a different color, it ruffled their feathers. Even though they got the new house along with the new furniture, they did not like to see their old house that they had cared for over so many years go through any changes. As a result, there were obvious struggles. As a child, I always thought that my grandparents were perfect people. They were Christians, and in my eyes, they could almost do no wrong. However, as I started becoming a teenager, I slowly noticed otherwise.

I remember overhearing an argument between my parents when I was about 12 years old. It was about my grandma. The next day, while my sister and I were walking together hoeing beans, I started to cry and told her that I feared that our parents were going to get a divorce. Divorce had started to be more common, and I would frequently hear my parents talk about couples whom we knew who were getting a divorce. My sister reassured me that they weren't going to separate. I was very relieved when later that evening my parents were talking and seemed fine. As a child, it is scary to think that your parents are going to separate. I remember having thoughts such as, "Who would I stay with permanently, my mom or dad?" or, "Would I have to leave my bedroom and our house for good and live elsewhere?"

As a teen, I wanted to fix everything. I wanted to fix the pain and disappointment that my mom felt as a result of living next to her in-laws. Even though I loved my grandparents very much, it would hurt me to see my mom in distress. I wanted to heal the heartache caused when my grandma sometimes called her fat or not smart. I didn't understand why my dad didn't defend my mom from the insults. Unfortunately, he would join in at times.

My grandpa would also occasionally make comments about my mom not being home very often. She was on the road a lot, but usually getting groceries or taking my brother to basketball practice. She was not going anywhere unrelated to her duties as a mother and homemaker. My grandparents were good, kind people but for some reason they felt the need to tell my mom what was on their mind too many times. I believe that is what caused the tension between my parents most of the time.

My mom had been an anxious and insecure child, and her insecurities sadly followed her into adulthood. This wasn't helped by the fact that, except for Marsha, she seemed to have little to no moral support. Although I was confident and secure as a child, as I grew older I think my mom's insecurities began to play on my mind and affect my own self-esteem. Being the one who always wanted to fix everything, when my best friend and I wouldn't agree on an issue, I would be the one to confront her about it and smooth things over. As I look back now, I don't know if I was simply being the more mature one or whether I was just insecure because I didn't want to lose a friend.

I don't think my insecurities really started until I got to middle school. This was during 7th grade in our school, although sometimes 6th grade is considered middle school in other areas. I had a lot of friends during elementary and into middle school. I was confident and had a good self-esteem. My parents and grandparents helped this by encouraging and praising me. They'd tell me how pretty I was and that I was very creative to be able to put outfits together, accessorize them and also decorate rooms. Even when I was very young, my grandma asked for my opinion on what articles of clothing looked good together. That would help me with my confidence. She would also ask for my opinion on decorating her house.

Living out in the country, we didn't have friends living close by where we could walk back and forth to each other's homes. My nearest friend lived 5 or 6 miles away. And my best friend since 2nd grade, Leah, lived at least 15 miles away. Leah and I had so much fun during our elementary years. She was an only child so she liked to come to my house where all of the action was. We always had my grandparents, cousins and uncle going in and out of the farmhouse on the weekends and summer.

Whenever she'd come over to my house, we'd watch *Three's Company*. We would sit on the carpet in front of the console television and roll with laughter at how funny John Ritter and Suzanne Somers were. She also loved to pester my brother. She would chase him around the house. Once she chased him while holding a bottle of Dawn dish soap while threatening that she would squirt it on him. I think maybe she had a little crush on him.

Leah soon became our Saturday shopping partner. While shopping we would get silly and try on gaudy dresses and model them for each other. She was almost like our own personal comedian! She was very witty. I could also confide in her about anything. She was a true friend. At the time, I couldn't imagine not having her as my best friend forever.

My family and I belonged to a nearby Lutheran church. It was the church my dad attended as a child. I later learned that my grandpa's parents helped build it. Every Sunday, my siblings and I went to Sunday school and every other Sunday we would all go to church as a family. I always thought it was normal that we only had a church service every other Sunday. I later learned that apparently it isn't! As it turns out, our full-time minister had moved on years ago and we had a temporary minister fill in who lived about 2 hours away. Hence the reason he only drove up every other Sunday for the service. This "temporary" minister ended up serving our community for many years. He's the only minister I ever remember seeing at my church.

I was always proud to say that I grew up in a church. However after going to my current church, I feel a different church could have made more of an impact on our lives. This wasn't a church where we could discuss our problems and ask for the congregation to pray for us. Unfortunately, at any given time, this wasn't a church we could ask for support from. We went to church, listened to the minister's stories about the Bible, and left. We didn't learn to have a relationship with God while outside of the church. We did not read the Bible at home or discuss much about it, or even pray. My family tried to treat others as they wanted to be treated and that was that. I didn't understand how we got to heaven when our time on earth was up. I simply believed that my family and I were good people so we would end up in heaven someday. I made mistakes and never asked for forgiveness. I didn't know I had to though.

It wasn't until my teen years that I started saying bedtime prayers. It started by me praying for help on a test I had the next day. Sometimes I felt it worked and other times I didn't. I guess I didn't really know how to pray or if there was a special way to do it. Also, were prayers actually answered?

My parents never gave me the feeling that they didn't enjoy being a part of and attending church. Although, come to think of it, they were never particularly excited about it either. Religion and church seemed to be the "done thing", a box we checked in a long list of activities that needed completing. It seemed that with farming, there was always something that needed to be done.

For this reason, we didn't go on too many family vacations. When we did, they were to places not too far away, like Cedar Point or Kings Island in Ohio. This was due mainly to my dad needing to be at home to work in the fields in the spring, summer and fall, and because my siblings and I were at school for the rest of the year. My parents went to Florida a few times on their own but it was during the winter months when farming wasn't an issue. However, when I was thirteen years old, we went on a road trip out West to Yellowstone National Park, visiting Old Faithful, Mount Rushmore and a zoo along the way. We also got to see our first rodeo, which was a lot of fun. This particular vacation was longer than most of our vacations, about ten days. I'm not sure why my dad decided to go out West but we enjoyed ourselves! My Uncle Ron, Aunt Nikki and their three boys joined us on our expedition, which made for lots of laughs. We stayed at hotels along the way and stopped every so often to eat and get gas. We didn't stay at the cheap motels on this vacation like we usually did. With Uncle Ron leading the way, he would stop at the nicer hotels with a swimming pool so we could swim in the evening. One of our funniest moments was stopping at a gas station that also sold hats. One of the hats had two bills, with one pointing to the right and the other to the left. On the front panel it read, "I'm the leader, which way did they go?" We laughed about that our entire vacation! We also couldn't stop laughing about the stack of pancakes my brother and cousin got at one of the restaurants we stopped at along the way. I think the stack was 8 inches high and the look on their faces was absolutely priceless!

It was a fun, interesting and educational vacation, filled with the kind of things that childhood memories should be made of. I vividly recall thinking to myself that one day, when I had a family of my own, I would make sure to take them on vacations just like this one.

I believe that the memories we make, the company we keep, the life lessons we're taught and the values instilled in us as we're growing up all form our roots. And just like with real trees and plants, these roots can either be shallow or deep. Our roots feed us and anchor us. Deep roots that are nourished and allowed to flourish hold us steadfast against the winds and storms of life. But when roots are shallow, a tree or plant can be easily bent or blown over. I feel that the roots of devotion to my family ran deep, as did the lasting memories of good times we had together. The shallower roots that were not given time and nurturing to be allowed to develop, particularly the roots of faith and self-esteem, caused insecurities that took hold and threatened the other, deeper, roots in my life.

> *"When the roots are deep, there is no reason to fear the wind."*
> *Chinese Proverb*

Patrick, Me & Connie, Easter 1989

Confirmation at church with mom & dad, 1991

CHAPTER 3
Broken

Bul·ly
boŏlē

Noun 1. *a person who uses strength or power to harm or intimidate those who are weaker.*
Synonyms: *persecutor, oppressor, tyrant, tormentor*
"he is a big bully"
Verb 1. *use superior strength or influence to intimidate (someone), typically to force him or her to do what one wants.*
"they bullied the younger boy into helping them"

Our school was very small, it had only 524 students from kindergarten through 12th grade in the year that I graduated. It got smaller over the years as people moved away because jobs became scarcer in the area. In 2017, the school closed its doors. It is sad to know the area you grew up in and where your family made a living is slowly becoming deserted.

    I happened to have an aunt, an uncle and a cousin who were all teachers at the school. This was difficult for me at times. I tried to be a perfect student because I didn't want them reporting any bad news to my parents. My dad's brother, Uncle Ron, was my 6th grade teacher. This caused me a lot of anxiety that year. On weekends when I wanted to relax and not think about school, my uncle would come over to help my dad on the farm and start quizzing me on the subject we were due to have a test on the following week. Maybe he was only trying to help, but at the time I didn't want to think about it. I hated taking tests and I felt the weekend was my time to enjoy myself and not think about school. Usually, if I had any homework to do, I'd do it on a Sunday afternoon.

Patrick and Connie were both honor students so I felt I had to follow in their footsteps. I spent a lot of time in my bedroom in the evenings during the week doing homework and studying. Math and studying did not come easily to me. I worked hard to be an honor student and ended up being third in my class. This probably doesn't say much given that it was such a small school, but I was still third in a class of 28 students.

Everybody knew each other at school. Sometimes this was a good thing, but at other times it wasn't. The upside of everybody knowing everybody else was that one could watch out for each other. However, I think rumors and gossip seem to get around much faster in a small community. Many of my friends' parents went to school with my parents so our parents knew each other well. I felt I could not do anything in that small town without someone finding out. Not that I had any inclination of being a wild teenager, but I felt as if I always had to watch my back and second guess whatever I did or said at school.

Six days after my 14th birthday, midway through 8th grade, I vividly remember getting off the bus one morning and going to my locker. My best friend, Leah, wasn't at my locker to greet me as she usually was. I turned the dial of the combination lock and opened my locker to hang up my coat and get my books for first hour class. There was a note in my locker that was apparently shoved through the vents. It was three folded pages with my name written in ink on the outside. It looked like my best friend's handwriting. As I opened it and read the words on that bright white lined paper, my heart started pounding. I started to shake and my face heated up. I could not believe what I was reading. I thought it was a bad joke. My best friend of six years had written to tell me that she didn't want to be my friend any longer. The note stated that she wanted to be in the "in" crowd. I was devastated. I didn't know what to do or who to turn to. I slowly walked with my head down to my first hour class, where Leah and I would normally sit next to each other. However, today, she was not sitting next to me. She was on the other side of the classroom where all of the popular kids sat.

I felt my world come crashing down around me. I held back my tears while trying to focus on the voice of my literature teacher. I could hear giggling behind me. Were they laughing at me? Were they talking about me? Why? I hadn't done anything wrong. After class, I caught up with a friend I'd had since 5th grade, Katie, and confided in her about the note. I didn't know what else to do. I felt I had to talk to someone about this unexpected betrayal. She consoled me. I felt I had to know that I could lean on her.

I tried to go on as if I wasn't hurt. I know that eventually I would have adjusted to not having Leah as my best friend and carried on with my life, but along with her rejection I now began to be horribly bullied. Leah soon became friends with four other girls who were mouthy, abrasive cheerleaders. They were popular with the boys and apparently that is what she wanted. The bullying happened so quickly. Unfortunately, since Katie was now hanging around with me, she also got bullied. As we walked down the hallway, the five girls would laugh and mock the way Katie and I walked. If I got called on to read a paragraph or two in class, the girls and more frequently the boys too, would giggle at the way I spoke and how I pronounced my words. Whenever I took a test and got the results back, they would look over my shoulder to see whether I got a good grade, and if I did they would call me a nerd. Whenever a teacher asked me a question in front of the class and I answered correctly, I was called a nerd. I got called a nerd so many times by them. I began to feel as though I shouldn't do my homework anymore, just so I would get bad grades and not have to face being called a nerd anymore. Were they jealous? Why was I a target? I couldn't do anything without getting a rude comment or laugh from one or all of the girls.

I had almost every class with those girls. It was as if they had their own little gang and it seemed to be getting bigger every day. Being a small school, the classes were small too so there was only one teacher per subject. There was never an option to change classes.

I recall making a metal tool box in shop class one day and had just finished spray-painting it red. One of the bullies sprinkled sawdust on the wet paint. I had to sand off the sticky paint and repaint my toolbox. I told the teacher what happened but the girl only got spoken to and not actually punished for her actions. This left me feeling very alone and unsupported.

The girls would also call me "Chinese eyes" and try to talk to me in a made-up foreign language to make fun of me. I never understood that because I never spoke Chinese. Maybe they were just so sheltered themselves that they didn't know that people come in many different shapes and sizes, and that everybody's physical features are unique? I think they were trying hard to find anything and everything to tease me about. My eyes were small, but that is how I was created. One wouldn't tease a person from China about their smalerl eyes, so why was I getting teased?

My anxiety levels soon started to increase and I became distant, almost like a hermit. I started to lose my confidence. I became anti-social and tensed up every time I entered a room with a large group of people. Even to this day, I still feel that way at times. I didn't want to go anywhere except shopping with my mom in the city. I knew that it was unlikely that I would run into any of the bullies there. I even stopped going to my brother's basketball games at school for fear of seeing these girls. When Friday afternoon would come around, I would get off the school bus, run into the house and finally relax from the week. I would feel as if a heavy weight had been lifted off of my shoulders. I could be myself, walk and talk the way God created me and not think about being bullied. Until the next week and it would start all over again.

During one of my brother's basketball games, my mom noticed the girls staring at her, talking and giggling. During half time, my mom ran into Deidra in the hallway. Deidra, who was actually one of my cousins, was the leader of the group of bullies. Her dad and my mom's dad were brothers. Deidra was very flirtatious with the boys and of course that's why the boys would side with her. She was tall, skinny and athletic and had boyfriends at a very young age. I recall her getting her first kiss on the lips from an older boy in 3rd grade. My mom, trying to help, told her to leave me alone. The following Monday at school, Deidra, along with the others, now had new ammunition against me, saying that I had to have my "mommy" fight my battles for me. No matter what I did or what anyone else did to protect me, it always seemed to make matters worse.

I know my mom meant well. I think she was tired of seeing my depressed, sad face come home from school day after day. She and my dad would call me grouchy. I did feel grouchy, and very depressed. School wasn't fun anymore and all I wanted to do was stay home in my bedroom where it was safe and no one could bother me or talk badly about me. Many days, I'd come home and lie on the couch or simply go to bed. I didn't know what to do or how to deal with what was happening to me. I didn't want to think about the bad day I'd had, I just wanted to close my eyes and dream about happy things. It was crushing to always be alone at school, to eat alone and sit alone. It was humiliating to not want to be selected to be on a team in gym class. Being the only one left when everyone else has been selected for a team, so they're "stuck" with you. I wasn't very athletic anyway but gym class wasn't fun for me, it was embarrassing. I used to like school, but now I absolutely dreaded it.

Soon after the bullying began, Katie got braces on her teeth and needed to go to the orthodontist quite often for check-ups. I would dread it when she would tell me that she wouldn't be in school for a portion of a particular day because she had an appointment. The night before, I would start worrying about what would happen the next day during school. She was the only one who sat by me in that large, loud cafeteria to eat lunch. When she was gone, I would go into my favorite teacher's classroom and either eat with her or eat alone if she had other lunch plans. It seems pathetic now but I felt safer by doing that.

Ms. Hunter was my English and Spanish teacher. She had a very positive influence on her students and was the kind of person who was compassionate and invested time and energy in her students. All of the students respected her. She was my adult support when I needed to talk to someone at school. Even though I had a cousin, aunt and uncle who were teachers there, I felt embarrassed to talk to them about being bullied. They had popular kids who nobody picked on and I felt like the unpopular, ugly, misfit cousin.

I don't know what I would have done without Ms. Hunter. I would ask her often, "Why am I the target?" Unfortunately she couldn't answer that for me. I don't think she really knew what to do either. And if she or another administrator ever spoke to the girls about their nastiness, it only made matters worse for Katie and me. We were then called narks. They would say, "Nark, nark, nark!" many times a day as they would pass us. I felt Katie and I were on our own to deal with what was happening and there wasn't anything we could do about it. It was two against many. We just had to deal with it. Looking back, I don't believe the teachers knew how bad it really was for us. It's easy to tell someone to just ignore the words and actions of a bully but it is very hard to actually do it.

Months went by and Leah still had not talked to me. Her mom, who was a friend of my mom's, called our house one Saturday morning. She wanted to get Leah and me together to try and resolve everything. I don't recall exactly what my mom told her but I do recall my mom telling her that Leah had initiated the conflict. Leah's mother was surprised to hear this as she had been told another story. She was under the assumption that I was picking on Leah and I was the one who had ended our friendship!

The following Monday, while in the girls' locker room getting dressed for gym class, the girls started bullying again. They said I cried to my mom and told her to call Leah's mom to beg for Leah's friendship back. I corrected them and let them know that it was Leah's mom who called my mom asking for us to try and sort everything out. They shut up for a little while. I tried to defend myself when I could but many times it was no use. The bullies didn't want to hear me.

The reality is that on many days, I did cry to my mom. I think she was lost too. She just didn't understand how Leah, someone whom she treated like another daughter, could turn on me and on her too. My dad and grandparents felt the same way. Leah was like another member of our family.

Unfortunately, the boys in my class sided with that group of girls. One of the boys tore up tiny pieces of paper and threw them in my hair. I snapped and scratched his arm with my manicured nails and made it bleed. I could only take so much of this abuse. At this point, I didn't care if I got disciplined. I wanted everything and everyone to stop! I felt I had no control any longer. I just wanted to be left alone. I had started acting out in retaliation sometimes, and it wasn't who I was. Many evenings I'd lie awake in bed thinking about the bullies and how I would love to physically attack them. I wanted them to feel some kind of pain. I wasn't feeling any physical pain, but the emotional pain was just as bad. In my eyes, these girls were so cold that they could never feel emotional pain, but maybe they could feel it physically. I recall walking into first hour class one day and having to do everything in my power to not attack Deidra. The day had only just started and I was already being called a nark as I walked down the hallway. I thought about pulling her long brown hair and dragging her out of that wooden desk. I was so angry and getting so frustrated with being teased. I felt like a bottle of pop which was being shaken and shaken constantly until it finally burst open and pop spewed out over everything. I was about to burst. I had to talk myself out of it. I knew the other kids would attack me if I started attacking her, and it would be my fault because I would have started the fight. I hated who I was becoming when I had to deal with these bullies. It wasn't me. I was not a mean girl or someone who would go around starting fights. I had to control myself. I felt lost, alone and out of control. I just wanted it to end.

I talked to the high school principal about what was happening to me. He talked to the girls. Apparently, the girls turned the story around and made it seem as if they were the victims. When the principal came back to me with this information, I was dumbfounded. I could not believe what I was hearing. Now the principal thought that I was making all of this up. It was their word against mine and Katie's. I felt hopeless. Once again, I turned to Ms. Hunter. She spoke to the principal and got it straightened out. I just could not believe that with all I was going through, I could not depend on my superiors for support. The principal should have asked more questions and asked other students to confirm who was telling the truth or not, before he came back to me with his thoughts. I was thankful I had kept Ms. Hunter in the loop with what had been going on.

Over time, a few high school students on my bus became

aware of what was happening to me in school. I vented to a couple of them one day. They started making the teachers aware what was happening to me. It didn't make a huge difference but it was a start. At this point, I was looking for any help I could get. I just could not believe that so few of the teachers were aware of what was going on. How could they not hear the snide remarks in class and as I walked down the hallway? How could they be so blind and oblivious? This was going on day after day. Where were they? I didn't understand why the girls weren't getting punished. I felt very alone in my despair, but I felt a little better knowing that some high school students had my back when they were nearby.

I would go to bed at night crying and praying. I didn't think that God heard my prayers though. I would ask myself, "What did I do to deserve this treatment? Am I such a bad child? Do I treat people this badly, somehow unaware of it, and now I am the one getting punished and 'paid back'?"

I just didn't understand. Was it because I didn't read the Bible or take church seriously and sometimes raised a fit on Sundays when my dad would make me go? Why me? Why was I getting bullied? These were the questions I asked myself many times.

Maybe it was because the bullies knew I'd be an easy target. I was soft spoken, short and not aggressive. I had self-confidence prior to being bullied. I always felt good about myself and would get many compliments. Now, I hated getting compliments from teachers. That would make matters worse for me. Whenever a teacher complimented me on a paper I wrote or even the clothes I wore, I'd get called a teacher's pet. No matter what I did, I was called something other than the name my parents gave me.

One day, I got so fed up that I mentioned to my chemistry teacher that I wanted to just kill myself. I was so emotionally tired of the bullying. After mentioning taking my own life, it was my teacher's obligation to call my parents. My dad answered the phone that evening. I don't believe he said a whole lot to the teacher. My dad confronted me about it afterwards and I said that I was just frustrated and would never take my own life. My dad believed me and apparently just blew it off because nothing else was said about it. I felt a little embarrassed that the teacher called my parents. If a child were to say that nowadays, they would probably be taken more seriously and possibly taken to see a therapist. Maybe that is what I actually needed, someone to take me more seriously.

I felt that at least if I were dead, I wouldn't have to go to school anymore and put up with the bullying all day. I felt that the pain would finally go away. Those girls could laugh about my death and move on to bullying someone else. I also used to wish that the girls who bullied me would die. I know that it sounds shocking, perhaps, but by this point I was beyond desperate in my desire to make it all end. If my dad had hand guns around the house, I believe I may have taken one or two to school. I admitted years later to Deidra that she would've been the first person I shot. At this point, I thought going to prison would be much better than going to school and putting up with them.

Logically, I knew taking my own life was not a good solution. I didn't hate my life that much but I did hate being at school. I know that it was the weekends and summer that helped get me through the awful times.

Interestingly, Leah didn't ever say anything horrible to my face. Instead, when others teased me, she would sit back and laugh. I think she was acting like a coward and deep down knew this was all wrong. There was no going back for her though. If she tried to be my friend again, she would get bullied. I just didn't understand how two friends who were as close as sisters and did everything together, could end up this way. I had confided in her about my dreams, my nightmares and even my crushes. She knew a lot about me and now her new friends probably did too.

That year seemed like five years. It went by so slowly. Summer finally came and suddenly I didn't have to worry about seeing any of them for three months. But another school year came and the bullying started all over again. I prayed that 9th grade would be different but it wasn't. Nothing changed. The girls didn't get any more mature. I wondered when God would humble them. Something had to change soon.

I recently came across this passage, Psalm 55:1-9, 12, 13. This describes me so perfectly during that awful time in school:

Listen to my prayer, O God.
Do not ignore my cry for help!
Please listen and answer me, for I am overwhelmed by my troubles.
My enemies shout at me, making loud and wicked threats.
They bring trouble on me and angrily hunt me down.
My heart pounds in my chest.
Terror of death assaults me.
Fear and trembling overwhelm me, and I can't stop shaking.
Oh, that I had wings like a dove;
Then I would fly away and rest!
I would fly far away to the quiet of the wilderness.
How quickly I would escape, far from this wild storm of hatred.
Confuse them, Lord, and frustrate their plans,
For I see violence and conflict in the city.
It is not an enemy who taunts me
I could bear that.
Instead, it is you - my equal, my companion and close friend[1].

The friction was getting the best of me and I felt just like the writer in Psalm 55:15-19, only I didn't think that the Lord heard my voice when I prayed.

> Let death stalk my enemies;
> Let the grave swallow them alive,
> For evil makes its home within them.
> But I will call on God, and the Lord will rescue me.
> Morning, noon and night
> I cry out in my distress,
> And the Lord hears my voice.
> He ransoms me and keeps me safe from the battle waged against me,
> Though many still oppose me.
> God, who has ruled forever,
> Will hear me and humble them[2].

Oh, I wanted them humbled so badly. I wanted someone to tease them and tell them they were worthless. I wanted them to second guess why they were born. I wanted them to get the evil butterflies in their stomach every time they entered the large brick building with the long hallway. I wanted them to ask, "What is wrong with me?"

Instead, I was constantly asking myself these questions. I was losing my confidence more and more each day. I realized that I didn't have to be liked by all of my classmates. I knew well that not everyone will get along. I could accept that perhaps people didn't like me but I couldn't accept being bullied. There was no reason to bully me simply because they didn't like me.

I did have a couple of other friends in my grade besides Katie. However, these friends were different. They would call me on the phone at night and we'd chat and laugh for sometimes an hour or two. Once in school though, they acted as if they weren't very good friends with me. I believe they liked me as a friend but not enough to stand up for me and be by my side. They knew that if they did, they would also be bullied by those girls. They saw what I was going through and they didn't want to go through it. I also had two other friends, one was a year older than me and one a year younger. Kerry, the one younger, also got bullied. Unfortunately, I wasn't in any classes with these two friends, so we couldn't support each other.

As the days went by, I used to wish that I could read their minds and understand why they were being such bullies. I wanted to find out what was so horrible in their lives so that they felt the need to bully me. I wanted to fix them but I couldn't. I felt I had no control of myself anymore. It scared me to think that I could even imagine taking my own life or one of theirs. I used to wish that I didn't belong to such a small school where there was just one long hallway and I would see the bullies daily. I wished my parents would pick up and leave the area. That was very unlikely though. I would dream about going to a new school and starting over. I imagined that, in a new school, I would try to change myself. I wouldn't be so shy and quiet. I'd try to be in the popular crowd yet be friends with the not-so-popular kids too. I knew that I wouldn't leave anyone out.

During 9th grade, Leah and I were assigned to work on a project together, and suddenly she started talking about the fun times we used to have. I think she really regretted doing what she did to me. But at this point, how could we go back? How would I ever trust her again? She even wrote me a letter asking to be my friend again. She wanted to know just how badly her and her friends treated me. I think during this time, Deidra was starting to shun her and moved onto other friends. I couldn't believe that Leah didn't realize how much she hurt me. Unfortunately, a couple of weeks later, Deidra started hanging out with Leah again and I was once again invisible in Leah's eyes.

Although I don't recall the exact details about how the

situation arose, sometime towards the end of 9th grade, Deidra and I found ourselves alone in a room together at school. Suddenly it all started to come out. She admitted that she was resentful of me. She was jealous that I had a good relationship with my parents and she didn't. She confessed things to me about her family which I would never have guessed. She confessed that she was jealous because I dressed nicely and got good grades. I was absolutely stunned. I didn't know what to say. I had heard it said before that "hurt people, hurt people[3]", which seemed to make sense in this case. Although I knew that that day was a turning point, Deidra had caused an awful scar on me. One that would take a long time to heal.

My 10th grade year arrived and I realized that I had been putting up with the bullying for two years. I knew this had prevented me from having a fun, normal, middle and high school experience. I would have liked to be a cheerleader but I felt that I couldn't with those girls on my squad. Dealing with them throughout the day was all I could handle. I was very anxious throughout those years, not only from being bullied but also due to the pressure I put on myself to get good grades and to make it into college. Being bullied was an added stress in school that was uncalled for. I was nervous enough to stand in front of my class to present a report but knowing I was going to get laughed at and made fun of made it more stressful. I could not wait until I graduated from high school. I never wanted to look back at those years and whenever I heard adults say, "Enjoy your school years while you can," I would cringe.

Midway through my 10th grade year, Ms. Hunter picked me, along with four other students, to start a group in school. It was called T.I.M, Teen Institute of Michigan. We attended a week's training at Central Michigan University, CMU. The training was statewide and provided information on alcohol, tobacco, and other drugs. We did group activities and team building to learn how to teach other teens that there are fun alternatives to these addictive substances. During this week, we learned a lot and it was a growing experience for myself and others. It helped me feel like a leader and it built some confidence in me. I felt very grateful to Ms. Hunter for including me in the group and giving me the experience.

I also joined a PAL® (Peer Assistance and Leadership) group. The mission of this nationally recognized program is to enable young people to use their potential to make a difference in their lives, schools and communities. I felt honored that Ms. Hunter suggested I join this group as well. I was always quite mature for my age and very understanding of others' feelings and needs. We learned how to help others in a crisis, be it drug abuse, problems with parents and other everyday teenage issues. I wish I had this training a few years prior, maybe it could have helped me get through the bullying time more easily.

After 10th grade, the bullying finally started to subside. Deidra wasn't in school often throughout her junior and senior year. She took classes at the local skill center. I also wondered how the bullies could go on with their lives and not look back on how they had treated me for so many years. They acted as if nothing happened or they did nothing wrong.

I feel your past can mold you into the person you will grow up to be, either in a positive or negative way. Even at 43 years old, I still feel the need to be liked by my peers and get distressed when I inadvertently upset someone, as I fear them turning other friends, coworkers and family against me. At times, I get paranoid and feel as if people are talking about me or laughing at me as they did in school. I lost my self-confidence from being bullied over the years and never got it back completely. Sometimes I feel the need to dissect what others are saying by asking myself things like, "Did they mean that in a rude way?" or, "Why did they say that?"

I have a concern that my daughters will be victims of bullying in school someday. I don't know yet what I will do if that happens. I know I would try to dig deeper to discover what background the bully has. I would make the principal and all of the teachers aware of it. One person cannot take on a bully or the bully's team. I currently tell my girls if they were to ever witness someone being bullied, to stick up for that person and to get their friends to also stand by for him or her. Having a more vibrant faith now than I did in my school years, I know that I would definitely pray about the situation earnestly.

As an adult, I am embarrassed to tell people that I was bullied as a child. I shouldn't be though. I feel as if people will judge me and not want to be my friend because they may see me as unpopular, not much fun to be around and just a plain loser. It's funny how the popularity status can even play out in the work force and not just in high school. On the flip side, I would hope that people I tell about my experience will not become my friend just because they feel sorry for me. The more I talk about being bullied to other adults, the more I'm finding that many adults have been bullied at least once in their lives. Many of these people are successful professionals who appear very confident.

Due to my past, it is so easy to feel a little stand-offish when someone is treating me kindly. I'm always questioning whether they have an ulterior motive. Are they nice because they want something or do they just want to mess with me and act like my friend so they can burn me later and laugh about it?

I fear having a close friend who might choose not to be my friend any longer for an unknown reason. Sometimes when I do make a friend, I expect something bad to happen that will destroy our friendship. I feel maybe I should do or say something to hurt them emotionally, before they have a chance to do it to me first. This, of course, is not healthy thinking. I have slowly come to learn that people will come and go in your life and sometimes there is no particular reason why. I believe that God just planned it that way. Unfortunately, not everyone will treat you the way you treat them and not everyone will put the same effort into the relationship that you do.

Many years later, I ran into Deidra at a relative's funeral. I don't recall how the subject came up, but she did not remember how she and her friends had treated me. She asked me with a puzzled look, "What did we do to you?"

I was in awe that she could not remember the cruel things they said and did. I remembered it as if it were yesterday. She apologized to me and it seemed as if she truly meant it. I don't think bullies realize or care how much of a negative impact they can have on a person while they are bullying them, and that this can play a profoundly negative role in the future for the victim. I've had trust issues since high school.

I also found out years after school that my brother's father-in-law was bullied by Deidra's dad while they were at school together. It was amazing to me that after about 50 years, his father-in-law still remembers being bullied.

I read an article once called, "*Bad Memories Easier to Remember*[4]". It stated that negative memories may be more vivid than happy ones. Negative events that cause emotions such as fear and sadness stimulate activity in the emotion-processing regions of the brain. These memories apparently are kept in greater detail than happy ones. The more often these emotional centers are activated by a negative event, the more you will remember specific details. This information helps prove why people remember where they were and what they were doing, including little details, when a tragedy happens. Many of us will remember exactly where we were when we heard about the September 11th attacks, or when we heard about a loved one dying, for example. Since reading this article I've been better able to understand why memories of the bullying as a whole, and specific events in particular, have never left me. Bullying left an undeniable mark on my life, the effects of which I am still living with today.

> *"The scars from being a victim of bullying may heal over time, but the trauma from the experience may never be forgotten."*
> *Ty Howard*

Why Don't You Like Me?

Why don't you like me?
What did I do to you?
Bully is your name,
When did you choose that to be you?

Why don't you like me?
Is it the color of my hair
or the shape of my eyes?
Is it the good grades I get and the failure of all your tries?

Why don't you like me?
Why do you talk so badly?
You don't know me and do not care
Why do you call me names
To those my thoughts I once did share?

Why don't you like me?
We're in the same boat
Just trying to make it through this stage of our life
While being a teen, going to school and trying to stay afloat.

Why don't you like me?
Why do you try so hard
To make me feel unaccepted,
Scared, with no support, and
And always feeling off-guard?

Why don't you like me?
Did I hurt you in some way?
Whatever I did,
I would not intentionally bring another to dismay.

Why don't you like me?
Don't you have a heart?
Put your feet in my shoes
Where no one is near
and everyone is far apart.

Why don't you like me?
Why do you giggle and smirk as I walk by?
It's as if you need to do it
To make yourself feel superior and high.

Why don't you like me?
Why can't this end?
Walk by as if I'm not there.
Continue forward and not be my foe or friend.

Why don't you like me?
Why won't you stop?
No one deserves this treatment
Just so you feel on top.

Brenda Fitzmaurice

CHAPTER 4
Branching OUT

Branch
bran(t)SH

Noun 1. *a part of a tree which grows out from the trunk or from a bough.*
Synonyms: *bough, limb, arm offshoot*
"I sat on the branch of the tree eating an apple"
Verb 1. *to bear or send out more branches.*
"this rose has a tendency to branch out"

My senior year eventually arrived. I had been longing for this time to come, knowing that soon I would be graduating and going off to college. By this time I was alone at home. Patrick had gone off to college and Connie had married her sweetheart, Ray, the previous summer.

Ray was liked by everyone. Even though he's 9 years older than Connie, they seemed to get along great and he easily fitted into our family. He acted just like "one of the boys" while playing basketball with Patrick and my cousins. Seeing Connie grown up and finding "Mr. Right" made me feel excited for her and made me think about my future. I would daydream often about what lay ahead for me. I had a lot to look forward to; college, a job, maybe even my own wedding someday.

Finally I was enjoying myself at school. I was doing the usual dating, going to football games and partying just like many of the teens in my town did. My parents kindly gave me their 1989 Buick Century that year and they bought a new car. My friend Katie and I would go shopping alone and to parties out at the pier or bonfires in the plains. We had so much fun!

I finally felt as though I fitted in during my senior year. Everyone was talking to me and not whispering or talking about me behind my back. I was actually going to school events. I was also dating a really nice guy and my parents seemed to like him too. I was able to really enjoy my senior trip during March of '93. Our class took a bus and went down to Florida, to Universal Studios, Cocoa Beach and Busch Gardens. I used to imagine all the fun I would have missed out on if I had taken my life. My senior year seemed to fly by compared to all the years I had been bullied.

I also didn't feel so stressed about my grades or taking tests. I figured my GPA was good enough at this point. During spring of my senior year, I had to finalize my decision on which college I wanted to go to. I thought a lot about a fashion merchandising school in Fort Lauderdale, Florida. I also toured the campus at Northwood University. Finally though, I decided on Central Michigan University. I got a small scholarship to CMU where I would study Interior Design. I was excited yet nervous about it. I was used to having my own space so sharing a dorm room with a stranger made me feel uneasy. I tried to stay positive though. I felt as if I'd been through so much during the previous few years. I had to keep telling myself that nothing could be worse than what I'd already been through and that I would do just fine at college.

My cousin, Marsha, designed the school yearbook every year. She was my art teacher in middle school and journalism teacher in high school and so I was able to get involved with the year book design during journalism class in my senior year. It was such a fun course and I felt that I could use my creativity. With it being a small school, we created one yearbook which included kindergarten through 12th grade. It was a very thin book but always turned out nicely.

> *"Living with fear stops us taking risks,*
> *and if you don't go out on the branch,*
> *you're never going to get the best fruit."*
>
> *Sarah Parish*

At the beginning of my senior year, I was told my GPA was 3.54 and that I was going to be in second place in our senior class, in other words I was going to be salutatorian. Throughout that year, I would check in with the school counselor to verify that I was still in second place. I wanted to stay on track and make my parents proud of me, as they had been of my brother when he was salutatorian. Around late March of that year, Marsha needed to get a definite answer on who placed where for the senior class GPA's. She needed to create that page in the yearbook. Marsha called the principal one Saturday to verify the order of the honor students. He reassured her that I was in second place.

A week went by and the school counselor announced that I was no longer second, but that I was now third in my class. I was absolutely devastated and couldn't understand it. What could have changed? By this time my grades had all been calculated and finalized, we had only three months left of school. There's nothing I could have done to make my grade come down that much and nothing the honor student in third place could have done to get that much ahead of me. It is still a mystery. My parents were very upset along with me. We just didn't understand.

My parents never went to school board meetings during my previous school years but my dad decided to go as a result of what had happened. He got some information from a board member that the father of the student who got bumped up to second place had just bought the school some new computers. Also, that student had nine other siblings who were either valedictorian or salutatorian in previous years. It seemed that the chain could not be broken. In our opinion, something didn't seem right about the whole situation.

This was just another let down during my school years in that small town. I guess I will never know what really happened. Did someone make a mistake in the calculations? Did someone lie? Did a parent pay the way for their child's step up?

My disappointment in not being made salutatorian was huge, but I knew that I had come up against worse situations before and survived. Making it through the endless years of bullying made me a much stronger person and I think that helped me get over the letdown of not being salutatorian. I knew now that I could make it through almost any negative circumstances I might face in the future.

Although the scars and wounds of bullying were still there, they were very slowly starting to heal, and each good day seemed a step forward in the right direction. I knew that God had allowed me to go through everything for a reason but I was not sure why. I felt as if I could see a light at the end of a very dark tunnel. As I grew in confidence, out of the darkness and into the light, I slowly started to branch out. I knew that soon I would be able to be more independent. I believed that God was finally on my side.

"If it should happen that your dreams are shattered,
Do not be afraid. Have the courage to pick
up the pieces and smile at the world.
For dreams that are easily shattered
Can just as easily be rebuilt."
Chris Jensen

The family at Pat's graduation

Me ready for Prom, 1992

CHAPTER 5
darkness

Darkness
därknəs

Noun 1. *the partial or total absence of light.*
Synonyms: *dark, gloom, dimness, murkiness, shadow*
"the room was in darkness"
2. *wickedness or evil.*
Synonyms: *evil, wickedness, sin, iniquity, immorality*
"the forces of darkness"

It was a typical Wednesday in April of 1993. My senior year was coming to an end and I was looking forward to heading off to college. I went to school, came home, ate the supper my mom had prepared and helped her with the dishes. We did not have a dishwasher; my mom was the washer and I was the dryer. It was our usual evening routine. Afterwards, I went upstairs to my bedroom, did my homework and was in bed by 9:30 p.m.

I was sound asleep when my mom came running upstairs around midnight, turned on my bedroom light and yelled, "Brenda!" I sat up quickly, startled.

"Guess what your dad just told me?"

My heart was racing as she recounted how my dad had confessed to her that he had cheated on her with Josie, my mom's brother's wife. After 25 years of marriage, he had spent the last two years having an affair with my aunt. My mom's brother, Bobby, was aware of this and hadn't told her what was going on. I could not believe what I was hearing. This had to be a nightmare. Meanwhile, my dad quietly came upstairs to my bedroom and sat on the edge of my bed. He couldn't look at me, he held his head low. I was crying and yelling, "Asshole, you asshole!" while hitting his arm with the palms of my hands. He still just sat, with his head in his hands, and couldn't look at me. He then left my bedroom and walked back downstairs to his. For some reason, my mom and I felt the need to call Marsha and tell her. She has always been my mom's "go-to person" whenever she needed advice or was going through a crisis and it felt natural to call her. Marsha was just as shocked as we were. She probably didn't think she heard me correctly on the phone when I told her the devastating news. It was late and I know I woke her.

My mom told me that she had to get out of the house for a while. I wasn't going to let her leave alone so I got out of bed and got dressed. We drove 45 minutes to my dad's sister Katherine's house in the middle of the night. We talked and cried the entire way. We could not believe that this was happening. Our perfect little family was going to be broken apart. We knew that this would forever change the way things had been.

We got to my aunt's house and knocked at the door. Of course she was fast asleep. As soon as she answered the door, she knew something was wrong, seeing the tears in our eyes and with it now being around 1:30 in the morning. We walked in and told her what had happened. She was shocked. My dad, her older brother, had always been a role model to her.

We talked practically all night and then finally lay down for a short while to try and get some rest, although I know that none of us could actually sleep.

The next day, Thursday, my mom and I went back to the quiet farmhouse while my dad was at work. We packed a few more clothes. We decided that I would go to Marsha's house to stay so Marsha could take me to school the next day and my mom would go back to Katherine's house.

Apparently my dad had a scheduled annual doctor's appointment that day. He confessed his wrong doings to the doctor and admitted that he hadn't been able to sleep. The doctor prescribed him some sleeping pills. My dad had also apparently been reading quite a bit about AIDS. In the early 80's this epidemic started spreading across America. I think my dad was paranoid about getting it due to cheating on my mom. I don't think he really understood how a person could contract the virus. The doctor ordered blood work as well to give him peace of mind.

On Friday, Marsha and I decided to play "hooky" from school. It was a beautiful day, we went for a couple long walks down her quiet road. We talked about what happened. She reassured me if my parents were to get a divorce, everything would be alright. Many couples divorced. Marsha herself had gone through a divorce and her kids were fine and had survived it. I felt a lot better but still in shock after hearing the news. How could my dad do this to us? Just thinking about it made me feel disgusted. Josie was not a typical pretty blonde with a skinny body. She was overweight with thin hair that barely got washed and teeth that seemed to never get brushed. She wore clothes that were too tight and shoes made for a man. How could my dad feel the least bit attracted to someone like her, someone who was the complete opposite of my mom?

Meanwhile, my mom went back to our farmhouse once again. She wanted to talk to my dad. She met him at the house after he did his mail route on Friday. He begged her not to divorce him. She agreed that she wouldn't, but wanted some time away to think things through. She was agonizing over what she had done to make him stray as he had. He also begged her not to tell his parents what he had done. Once again, she agreed to his requests and told him that this news would kill his mother and she wouldn't want to do that.

He was an embarrassed and ashamed 50-year-old man who didn't want to let his parents down. He had never been a rule-breaker and had always seemed to have very high morals. He did not want his parents to find out that he had disappointed them and shattered his family.

My grandpa had been in and out of the hospital in recent months due to heart issues. This seemed to have really been stressing my dad out. I think he was worried that if something were to happen to his dad and also his mom, then he couldn't farm all of their land on his own or otherwise that he would have to pay out his two siblings for their part of their inheritance. On Friday night my dad went to his brother's house so that they could ride together to visit their dad in the hospital. My dad confessed to his brother and sister-in-law that evening about his affair and told them that my mom and I had left him. My Aunt Nikki talked to him, urging him to give my mom and me time to handle this shocking news and not to do anything drastic.

Sadly, her plea fell on deaf ears. My dad returned home that evening to an empty house. He got a pen and a piece of paper and began writing. He generally had very precise, neat handwriting, so I can only imagine that his hand was shaking quite badly as he wrote.

> Dear Charlotte & Kids,
> I always love you and I gave the kids more then any around. I want to go where dad is going. There are beans & wheat stored in the elevator. There are life Insurances. You are set pretty good.
>
> Good bye
>
> GAry

After writing the note, my dad took a few of the sleeping pills which the doctor had prescribed. He walked out into our garage and started his 1972 pickup truck. He then got into his white Subaru mail car, started it and reclined the cushioned blue seat while the doors and windows were tightly closed. He drifted off to sleep around 9 p.m. and never woke up.

I have never been able to get over the fact that, in his final moments, as he wrote that note, my dad was thinking of our financial well-being when he should have been thinking about never ever seeing us again. Oh how I wish that he had gone in the living room instead and looked at the 8x10 wooden framed school pictures of me and Connie and Patrick on the wall. Perhaps he would have rethought what he was about to do and called someone for help? He could have called his co-worker, Lillian, who knew he was having problems, or he could have called his brother. What was he thinking?

Lillian, the postmaster at the small post office where my dad worked, had apparently noticed approximately a year prior to his death that he had been a little down in the dumps. A month before, he had finally confided in her and told her of his affair. She could tell that he felt awful about it and that he needed help. She had told him that people stray and that it wasn't the end of the world. She had called for support from their Grand Rapids location and got some information for my dad and some details on counseling options in the area. I will always appreciate the way she tried to help. He chose not to get any professional help though. My dad also told her that he confessed to my mom and that she and I had left the house on Wednesday night after the confession. Lillian said he had been really distraught on Thursday but by Friday, he seemed to be in a good mood. She said she had been so happy to see that the old Gary was back. She called my dad on Friday evening just to make sure that everything was fine. He lied to her, telling her that everything was ok and that my mom was there with him. She had thought about going to our house anyway but did not want to intrude, especially if my parents were working everything out. Oh how I wish she'd gone over.

Meanwhile, my friend Katie and her boyfriend were in the area and drove by the brightly lit farmhouse. They thought about stopping to see if I was home. Katie knew by then about my dad's infidelity and knew my mom and I were having a difficult time absorbing the news, so they decided instead to drive on. I wish they had driven into the gravel driveway and heard the truck and car both running in the garage. Perhaps they could have saved my dad.

Saturday morning arrived and although it was after 8 a.m., my dad had not yet shown up for work, which was very unusual for him. Lillian called my dad's brother, Ron, and asked him to go to our house and check on my dad. Ron was puzzled and got in his vehicle immediately and drove out to the farm. He walked into the empty house to the sound of the TV blaring. Immediately, he saw the note on the dining room table. He rushed to the master bedroom yelling, "Gary! Gary!" He yelled up the flight of stairs, "Gary, Gary!" He went outside and stood on the sidewalk and it was then that he heard a vehicle running. He rushed into the garage to find that the old '72 truck had been running all night. He opened the door of the mail car to find my dad reclined on the front seat. He tried to give him CPR but it was too late.

Ron called my Aunt Nikki to tell her to call the ambulance. Nikki was shocked to hear that my dad was dead. She did what she was asked to do, but she couldn't remember the address of our house to tell the officer. Coincidently, the officer knew Nikki and her family and knew our address and was able to send the ambulance.

At around 9 a.m. at Marsha's house the phone began to ring. Marsha's friend was on the line asking, "What is going on at Char's house?"

She said that she heard on the police scanner that an ambulance was called out to the "Gary Huber" residence. Marsha immediately hung up the phone and called my grandma's house to see if Ron was there. When she couldn't reach anybody, she called Ron's house. She talked to his son and asked where he was. He said that his dad had gone out to the farm. This wasn't unusual because on many Saturdays, Uncle Ron would come to our house to help my dad farm.

I was sitting in Marsha's living room and I could hear the panic in her voice. She was saying over and over, "Oh no, oh no".

I kept asking her, "What's wrong?" but she wouldn't answer me.

Marsha could sense something was horribly wrong. She dialed our home phone at the farm. My uncle answered the phone and Marsha asked him, "Is Gary alright?"

Ron replied sadly, "No. Keep Brenda at your house for now."

He wanted to be sure my dad's body was gone before we

got there. They were waiting for our family doctor to arrive to officially pronounce my dad dead along with a specific time. The officials believed he actually passed at 11:30 p.m. Marsha hung up the phone and quietly told me what had been said. I fell to my knees on her shag carpet and cried and cried, yelling and pounding the floor with my fists. This was another nightmare! Was this really happening? It felt as though I was living in a horror movie.

The ambulance drove into the large driveway of our farmhouse that morning. My grandma, living next door, saw the ambulance pull in. She sensed something was wrong. She left her house and ran through the garden yelling, "Gary, Gary!"

It was as if she knew something awful had just happened. Her own father had committed suicide when she was only a young woman of 25. She was reliving that awful nightmare, but it was not her father this time, it was her son.

Uncle Ron then called Aunt Katherine, where my mom was still staying, and told her what had happened. My mom was standing next to Katherine when she got the call. My mom saw her face turn deathly pale and asked, "What's wrong, Katherine?"

Katherine hung up the phone and told my mom the news. Mom started shouting and crying hysterically. Aunt Katherine called my brother to give him the news. He drove to her house to pick up Mom and take her home. They drove as fast as they could. Maybe they thought if they drove fast enough, they could still somehow save him?

Marsha and I finally got the confirmation to go to my house. When I got there, my mom and brother were already there, and my sister and her husband were on their way. I gave my brother a big hug in the entry of the house. Then I walked into our kitchen where my grandma was sitting in the wooden dining chair, staring out of the window. It was as if she was somewhere else. She wasn't crying though. She was being strong for us and holding it in. I hugged her while crying, "I don't have a dad anymore."

"No, you don't," she replied softly.

That day seemed to last forever. My mom and Marsha made many phone calls. My friend Katie came over to console me and spend the night. She slept on my bedroom floor while I cried myself to sleep in my bed.

During the night, something really strange happened, although it was so real and so vivid at the time. I am unsure whether I was actually awake when it happened, or perhaps I was dreaming? In the middle of the night I saw a large hand come through my window. The hand patted me on my shoulder, as if to say, "It's going to be alright, everything is alright." I could physically feel this touch, but I wasn't afraid.

At the time, I thought maybe it was my dad's hand trying to console me. As I look back now and as I've come to know more about God over the years, I know it was his hand reaching out to me and comforting me. In the middle of probably the darkest night of my entire life, I can honestly say that I felt great comfort, and have never forgotten this vision, experience, or whatever else one might call it. It was so real to me.

I was so grateful for this measure of comfort. My thoughts were so scattered, racing around in my head. I was trying to relive moments and conversations I had had with my dad over the previous few weeks and months. I hadn't noticed any signs that he was so depressed, or maybe I simply overlooked the signs? My mom didn't see any signs of his depression either. He didn't talk about his feelings much and he was always so busy. I can only imagine the darkness he found himself in.

I do recall a year earlier my dad was talking about an acquaintance of his (another farmer in the area) who had taken his own life. However, this farmer shot himself. Holding his thumb and pointer figure to his head, I can remember my dad telling me that he would never have the nerve to pull that trigger. He said that he would just put the old truck and car in the garage. He told me that older vehicles will stay running unlike the new vehicles nowadays with their catalytic converters which will prevent them from running too long. Maybe he was crying out for help then but I didn't notice. I thought we were just having a casual conversation about an acquaintance of his.

It's so natural to blame God and ask, "Why weren't you there for my dad? Why didn't you stop him or make him realize there are other options and people who could help?"

I try to imagine what my dad was thinking or feeling when he went into the garage for the last time, as he started the vehicles and reclined the car seat and waited to fall asleep. Were there tears prior to drifting off or were there thoughts of relief that the pain and guilt would soon be over? There had to have been a few minutes before the sleeping pills kicked in where he was thinking about something or someone. God gives us free will, but it is hard and always will be hard for me to understand how our God, who is so good and supposed to protect us, could allow this to happen to my family. I have asked myself so many times over the years, "Why didn't God use his power to stop this act? Why didn't he use a neighbor or friend to stop it?"

My dad didn't give us an opportunity to talk with him about why he cheated on my mom. He took matters into his own hands very quickly. He felt ashamed. I later read that shame is feeling that *'I am something bad'* and guilt is *'I did something bad'*. Satan uses both shame and guilt to make us feel unworthy and unloved. I can only imagine the battle going on in my dad's mind as he wrestled with these feelings of worthlessness and darkness. Sadly, in this case, Satan won the battle.

"Suicide is a permanent solution to a temporary problem."
Phil Donahue

CHAPTER 6
battered
BY THE STORM

Storm
stôrm

Noun 1. a violent disturbance of the atmosphere with
strong winds and usually rain, thunder, lightning, or snow.
Synonyms: tempest, squall, gale, outburst 2. a tumultuous reaction;
an uproar or controversy. "the book caused a storm in America"
Verb 1. move angrily or forcefully in a specified direction.
"she burst into tears and stormed off"

On Sunday the gathering started. Aunts and uncles, great-aunts and great-uncles, cousins and neighbors all started showing up, bringing their condolences and lots of food. The word was getting out about our loss. The community and family were shocked and saddened. My dad was well liked by everyone he met. He was kind, quiet and sincere.

That day my mom, my brother and I went to the funeral home to pick out my dad's casket and drop off the clothes my mom picked out for my dad. She chose his gray pants and navy-blue sports coat that he wore to church on Sundays. I held back my tears as best I could. I wanted to be strong for my mom. We chose a dark brown casket with cream colored interior and a picture of wheat on the inside of the lid. The wheat seemed fitting given that he was a farmer. We sat with the funeral director to write his obituary. I remember thinking that this was something I should never have to do at the age of 18. With the help of the director we were able to complete it as best we could. It went like this:

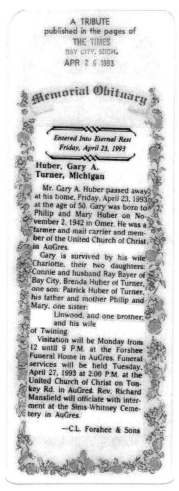

On Sunday evening the viewing at the funeral home began. It continued through Monday and many people attended. It was all so overwhelming. I wished that my dad could have seen all the sad faces of those who knew him.

Maybe he would have realized that he was respected, loved and adored. Maybe he would have realized that among all the people who showed up, at least one of them could have helped him.

My mom had a break down by the time Monday evening came. I was in another room and saw my mom through the large doorway on the floor in front of the casket, crying and pounding the floor. I think she broke down after she saw her brother's son show up. Maybe it was just too much for her to handle. She had lost her husband and was now a widow at the age of 46, and she felt she had lost a brother too. As a family, we had made it clear that her brother and his wife were not allowed in the funeral home to see my dad.

It was a really difficult two days and I was not looking forward to Tuesday, the day of the funeral. I knew that it would be the last time I ever saw my dad's face, except for in the few photos we had of him.

Throughout all that was going on over the previous few days, my grandma had been back and forth to the hospital visiting my grandpa who was unwell again. On Monday, my grandma and my great-aunt, Betty, were in my grandpa's room at the hospital when Betty noticed that my grandma had started slurring her words. She also started telling Betty that her left arm had a tingling feeling in it. Betty quickly ran to get a nurse. The nurse assisted my grandma into a room next to my grandpa's. She was clearly having a stroke.

As we were getting ready for the funeral on Tuesday, we received a call from my uncle to say that my grandma had passed away. I recall sitting in my brother's room and hearing my mom on the phone downstairs. All I could think to say was, "Poor Grandma." I really believe she died of a broken heart.

My grandpa took the news pretty well, all things considered. He knew his wife wouldn't be able to live without her eldest son. They were like two peas in a pod - they acted alike and thought alike. The only thing my grandpa could say was, "My good boy."

It was an awful day. Our immediate family went to the funeral home early before other family and friends showed up. We chatted with each other about the recent news of my grandma's passing. We were again saddened and shocked. We could not believe this was happening to us. How much more could our family handle?

We were there to pay our last respects to my dad before the men in dark suits shut the casket forever. I stood up by his side hoping he'd wake up. I didn't want them to close the casket just in case he did. I had to touch him one last time. The last time I had touched him, I was hitting him and calling him "asshole." Finally, I got the courage to touch his cold, stiff cheek. It was the first time I had ever felt a corpse. It wasn't what I expected. It felt so hard. I really didn't know what to expect though. He was unusually white, and he had always had a wonderful tan complexion thanks to hours spent in the sun driving his tractors. I wished that the funeral cosmetologist could have put darker make-up on him so he looked more natural and more like himself. His prominent cheek bones weren't so visible anymore. His face didn't look as long and narrow as it once did. It looked rounder. I kissed his cheek as my uncle hurried me along so that others could see him for one last time. I wasn't ready to leave that soon but I did.

We drove the few miles from the funeral home to our little Lutheran church. It is such a pretty church, sitting at the intersection of two country roads, with its white walls and tall steeple. We took our seats in the front pew of the church. I sat there while the pall bearers carried the large casket down the aisle of the little church and placed it, with a beautiful flower arrangement on top, directly in front of me. The church started getting more crowded as the people began to file in. It was a sunny day, I could see the sun streaming through the stained-glass windows. Eventually there were too many people in the church. Friends, family, class mates of mine, even the bullies, were sitting and standing everywhere. Some were inside and others were outside trying to look in from the paved landing of the church.

As I sat with the casket within touching distance, my knees started to shake uncontrollably. My mom was sitting on one side of me and my sister on the other side. I longed for my knees to stop shaking and I longed for someone to hug me and tell me that everything was going to be okay. My sister looked at my mom and pointed to my knees. I'm not sure if she just didn't know what to do, or whether she was shocked that my knees were doing what they were, seemingly with a mind of their own. I wanted to be able to cry loudly and let it all out. I wanted to yell, "Come back to us, wake up!"

But I knew this wasn't the time or place to do that while everyone else talked in whispers around me.

Our minister seemed to talk forever. I didn't really hear what he was saying even though he was standing almost directly in front of me. If I had to guess, he probably said something like this: "Gary was a good husband, father and son. He was a giver and hard-worker. Following in his father's footsteps, he was a farmer for his entire life. He was also a dedicated and reliable mailman. He yearned to always make his parents proud. He cared about others and would give the shirt off his back to a stranger if they needed it. He was humble when he did well and tough on himself when he made a mistake. He loved his wife and kids and was so proud of all of them. He had a good sense of humor and liked to joke around and have fun. He attended church regularly and loved the song 'The Old Rugged Cross'."

After the service, my brother drove my mom and me while following the black hearse to the cemetery. My sister and her husband were in a car behind ours. The grave had already been dug, waiting for the casket to be lowered into it. We sat in the chairs that were placed around the gravesite and listened to the minister say his last prayers. This would be it.

There was no coming back to earth for my dad. Even if he did wake up and this was some kind of cruel joke, he was going to be buried six feet under! It was only the memories and pictures that we would have of him now. Unfortunately, the last memories were not very good ones.

When we arrived back home, I think we were all still in a daze. Was this really happening? I remember thinking to myself, "Is he really not going to walk through that kitchen door anymore?" The house already seemed empty. My brother cracked open a Bud Light and I did too. I wasn't 21 yet but my mom didn't object. I felt as if I was too tired to cry anymore. I knew I didn't want to think about it any longer and my brother probably felt the same. That beer actually relaxed me and tasted good. I thought to myself that I should have drunk it before going to the funeral.

In less than a week, we would be doing this all over again for my grandma. It was really hard to mourn for her while we were mourning my dad, still in shock over the news of his infidelity, and then his awful choice of suicide.

It was amazing to hear people at the funeral home tell us that they were there for us and that if we needed anything, to let them know. Once the funeral was over though, I felt like asking, "Where did everyone go?"

When you lose a loved one, during the first few weeks, it feels as if you are going through a crazy maze blind-folded. When you are home and realize that person is gone forever and will not be walking through the door again, you feel empty. No one is around to talk to. All the well-meaning people who were at the funeral continue to live their lives as if nothing happened. The saying, "Life goes on" becomes very real.

It just wasn't fair. I would hear strangers laughing in the stores and on the streets and I would think, "How can they be so happy?"

I couldn't find anything to laugh about and neither could

my mom. I honestly do not know how my siblings were dealing with the losses. We never talked about it, but I was having a hard time with it. Maybe I was having a harder time because I was still living at home whereas my brother and sister were off living their own lives.

I missed a week of school that senior year going back and forth to the funeral home. When I did go back to school, I was shocked by the way my peers came up to me to offer me their condolences. I would think, "These people didn't talk to me prior to my loss, why are they talking to me now?" I guess peoples' hearts can warm to one when a tragedy hits. There were some however who started rumors. I guess there usually are rumors when people don't know the facts or understand a situation. A classmate announced that he heard that my mom cheated on my dad, so that's why he killed himself. I mostly managed to ignore rumors like those and I learned that I had little respect for those spreading them.

Prior to being off school due to the funerals, we were assigned to write about euthanasia in speech class. Euthanasia is assisted suicide and is usually as a result of someone suffering from a terminal illness. I recall my teacher asking me if I wanted my paper back when I returned from my time off. I took it and waited until I got home to reread it. It was hard because what I believed while I wrote the paper was so different to how the past week had played out. I did believe that if a person was suffering with a terminal disease, that they should be able to ask for assistance in taking the suffering away. I did not believe that someone who is physically healthy should get assistance or take it upon themselves to end their life. I neglected to mention in my paper my thoughts about being mentally unhealthy. I feel there can be a cure for mental illnesses with therapy or medication. Many people live with a mental illness and survive. My dad should've gotten help.

I am still heart broken when I see people fight for their lives due to cancer or some other illness. Many people fight long and hard to live because their life was once happy. Then I think of my dad who had a good life, who was physically healthy and who could enjoy his time on earth, but decided to rather just give up and take his own life. To this day, I often need to remind myself that he was ill too, maybe not physically ill but he was very definitely mentally unwell.

My dad's doctor's office called regarding his blood work about a week after his death. They wanted him to go back in to get it done again due to someone spilling the blood at the lab.

My mom had to tell them that he was no longer with us. We always thought it to be somehow unusual that the blood got spilled. At this point though, there was nothing anyone could do about it. If he had a disease, we would never know. We just hoped that nothing had spread to my mom.

My mom had so much guilt. She blamed herself for my dad's death. She tried to remember if there were any signs that my dad was trying to show her how unhappy he was. She does recall that he once said that maybe he should see a therapist. My mom just shrugged it off, assuming he was goofing around and talking nonsense. Maybe he was trying to cry out for help. My mom assumed everything was fine between them. She had no idea what was going on. It was so easy to blame myself and others for his suicide. I had to keep telling myself that his act of suicide had no reflection on me. I could not blame myself or others. I think I just wanted some kind of concrete answer as to why he did it. I yearned for a written answer in black and white as to what caused him to take his life. What was he feeling? How come he didn't reach out to anyone? Why was he hurting so badly? I remember thinking to myself over and over again that suicide is so final. And yet it's also not a solution.

April turned into May and I was looking forward to Prom.

The guy who I had been dating since summer of the previous year took me. We had a nice time. We danced and hung out with friends. It was great to have a reprieve from all the sadness at home and to just be a normal teenager for one night. I was voted Prom Queen which really surprised me. I still wonder if people voted for me because they felt sorry for me or because they truly wanted me to be Queen. I guess I will never know.

Graduation day was particularly hard. I walked down the road to my grandpa's house with my cap and gown on so he could see me in it. He was currently home from the hospital but not doing very well so he didn't attend my graduation ceremony. We got my mom to take a picture of us together and to this day, my eyes get watery when I look at it. He looked so frail.

The ceremony at school went well. I tried to hold back my tears, not because of leaving school and the fear of being on my own, but because three people I loved so much weren't there. Maybe it was a blessing in disguise that I was not salutatorian, I would have had to make a speech that evening in front of a few hundred people. I don't think I would have been strong enough to stand at the podium with a clear voice and dry eyes. I kept thinking about all I'd been through, as I sat and listened to the valedictorian and salutatorian speeches. I felt as if I had been to hell and back and survived it. Heck, my future and college should be a breeze compared to what I've been through, I thought.

I felt like a tree that had been battered by a storm. I remember during one particularly awful summer storm looking out my window on the farm, at my beloved lilac bush in the corner of the yard. It was so windy outside that the bush was being bent this way and that, assaulted by the gale. Eventually we had to head down into our basement for safety. I knew, however, that my lilac bush would survive. Even though it looked like it couldn't possibly stand up to the tempest much longer, it had thick, strong, deep roots and I knew that these would help it to survive despite what seemed like the harshest of circumstances. I knew that my deep roots would hold me strong once again and that I would survive this storm.

> *"I'm thankful for my struggle because without it I wouldn't have stumbled across my strength."*
> *Alex Elle*

My senior picture

Senior Prom, 1993

Graduation Day

My grandpa & me
My senior graduation 1993

CHAPTER 7

Growth
grōth

*Noun 1. the process of increasing in size.
Synonyms: development, progress, headway,
movement, advancement
"the upward growth of plants"
2. Something that has grown or is growing.
"a day's growth of unshaved stubble on his chin"*

In June 1993 I graduated from high school. We went ahead with my graduation party as planned. It was held at our house, in the garage where my dad had taken his life. Most of my family came to celebrate with us. Of course though, there were two people missing from that celebration and it just was not the same having a celebration like this without them.

My mom and I went through all the emotions of losing a loved one. We felt angry that he had wanted to leave us and that he had gone ahead with it. We felt sad and depressed. We felt guilty. Perhaps we should have stayed at the house instead of leaving him? We also felt sympathy towards him, for what he must have felt and how badly he must have been hurting to do what he did. My mom also felt betrayed.

Now with my dad gone, my mom did not want me to go to CMU anymore. She wanted me to go to a college closer to home. So instead of the interior design course I had planned to start, I registered to take general classes until I finalized my major at SVSU, Saginaw Valley State University. Although this wasn't what I had planned, I felt it was the best decision. I knew that I would be close enough and available if my mom needed me.

In August, just before starting college at SVSU, my grandpa passed away at the age of 72. He was now with my grandma and dad. I've heard it said before that deaths run in threes.

By this stage, I could not wait until 1993 was over. It was the worst year of my life and I hope I never have to go through another one like it. There's a little superstitious side of me that recalls me breaking my locker mirror at the beginning of 8th grade. Did that have anything to do with my bad luck? Also, a couple of years before, my mom was decluttering an upstairs closet prior to my dad passing away and came across her wedding dress. She had always heard that giving away your wedding dress is bad luck. She thought that being married for 25 years, what could happen? So she gave it to Goodwill. Is that what brought on all of our troubles? Although I knew by now that these were just frivolous coincidences, maybe I wanted some concrete answers as to why everything we had gone through as a family had happened. I guess that, this side of eternity, we will never know why God allowed what He did. I truly believe now that God could have stopped all of it, but He chose not to. They say that God does not give you anything you cannot handle – my family and I must be very strong humans!

On top of everything else, I found out that my senior year boyfriend cheated on me with one of my classmates during the summer after graduation. I was distraught but I knew I would make it through. I couldn't believe it though because he knew how I felt about infidelity – I had shared with him about what my dad did to my mom, and yet he still did it to me! This felt like a blip in the road compared to everything else though. I surprised myself by picking up and moving on. I had grown in confidence and knew that there must be someone better out there for me.

The summer after high school, I started hanging out with Michele. She was one of the girls from the group of girls who bullied me. We found out we had more in common than we thought. We decided to get an apartment together and attended college together only an hour from our farmhouse. I could easily and frequently go home on weekends to see my mom. I finally got up enough courage to ask Michele what went through her mind as the other girls were bullying me as she just stood by. She said, "I was just glad it wasn't me getting picked on for once, especially about being overweight."

It was helpful to have an explanation of some kind for her involvement in the bullying. More and more I began to realize that all the girls who had been involved in that group had a painful story that I knew nothing about.

My mom was having a difficult time living in the large farmhouse alone. No one was walking through the door any longer to just see what was happening on the farm. She had to become more independent, had to be responsible for the house, the yard and paying all the bills. These responsibilities had always fallen on my dad. One weekend evening while I was home from college, my mom all of a sudden became hysterical. She kept saying over and over that she wanted to go where my dad was and that she didn't have a reason to live anymore. It was as if she lost all control of her body, just as she had done that evening in the funeral home. At the time I didn't know what it was, but now I recognize it as a nervous breakdown or perhaps even a panic attack. I didn't know what to do so, as usual, I called Marsha. She came over immediately and helped to calm Mom down. I knew that I wouldn't be able to handle my mom killing herself too. I was angry that she could even say these things, knowing the difficult time we were already going through.

Mom felt a significant void in her heart and soul. She had lost the only love of her life. She was with him for 25 years and then suddenly, he was gone. She never seemed like her old self after my dad died. I know she felt desperately alone whenever she had to attend a family wedding or outing by herself. She was envious of the other couples dancing happily together. She felt envious of couples retiring together and traveling. That is something she and my dad use to talk about and dream about doing once he retired from farming. Now, she couldn't even concentrate and sit down long enough to read a book as she once used to enjoy doing. She didn't want my dad's insurance money or the large farmhouse, she only wanted my dad. She would have been satisfied without the money and material items if she could only have had my dad back.

My mom later leased out the farmland to my dad's cousin and sold the farm equipment. She bought a home in Florida and moved there, but sold it within a few months and came back to Michigan. It was almost as though she didn't know which direction to go in for a few years. Eventually, she ended up selling the farmhouse and moving to the city to be near my sister, Connie, and her husband, Ray. My brother was in college so he couldn't take over the farm. There were too many memories in that house and it was just too large for one person. I was saddened to know that the farmhouse would no longer belong to my family. My kids would never know the house I grew up in, and never see the bedroom that was my "safe" place. They would never have a chance to climb in my favorite lilac tree. Despite all this though, I knew this was the best decision for my mom. Since my mom sold the house, I have tried to drive past once a year on the way to the cemetery where we laid my dad to rest. The new owners have done a good job of keeping it up, with new improvements made every so often. It feels good to think that my childhood home is well loved by another family now.

During this time, my anxiety started to return. Whenever a day went by and I didn't hear from my mom, I became paranoid that she too had decided to take her life. I would then call my sister or brother to ask if they had heard from her. Sometimes I even called Marsha to see if she had talked to my mom that day. Cell phones weren't as available then so all we had were landlines. When I started to feel worried, there was no easy way of tracking my mom and making sure that she was ok. This only added to my fretting.

My mom and I started seeing a therapist prior to her moving to the city, although overall it wasn't a good experience. I thought it would be helpful to talk through my past, the bullying I'd experienced, and to talk about how to deal with my dad's suicide. It was a relief to be able to talk to an outsider about what had happened in my life. It felt good to just breakdown once in a while. I told the therapist that I had had a good childhood and then I told her everything that had happened to my family in the last year. For some reason though, she became overly focused on my relationship with my dad. She continued to tell me about herself and how her dad had molested her. I made it clear that my dad did no such thing to me. I told her that my dad had missed a few of my dance recitals and would go to my brother's basketball games. I understood why though, since my recitals were often during planting time whereas Patrick's games were during the winter months when Dad was not working in the fields. The therapist had the boldness to tell me that apparently my dad had loved my brother more than he had loved me. I was furious! I immediately stood up, walked out of her office and never went back. I knew that what she said was not true. My dad loved me and my siblings equally. I was always daddy's little girl and as we grew older, my siblings would tease me and say that he spoiled me.

A few months later, my mom went through a phase of visiting various bars in the evenings. I know she was just looking for company but I would worry about her. I worried that she would be drinking and driving, or that she would meet a stranger who wasn't any good for her. She did eventually meet a man at one of the bars who she started dating on a regular basis. My siblings and I thought it was good for her. We hated seeing her alone and not having a companion to do things with.

He became a great friend and helped her move on with her life and make it as normal as it could be. My mom had always been very active in sports in her earlier years so he got her golf lessons which she really enjoyed. They went on a few vacations together and she grew to love his family. She was with him for seven years and later realized it was unfortunately a few years too many. He started to drink a lot and talked disrespectfully to her. He didn't like me and my siblings much because we used to tell him when we thought he wasn't being considerate towards our mom. It really upset us though when he tried to convince my mom to change her will and put his name on her house. My dad's hard-earned money had bought her that house in the city, and we were furious to think that he was trying to get his hands on it. My siblings and I tried to convince my mom to leave him and that she didn't deserve to be treated as badly as he treated her. She had no obligations to him, we told her that it would be an easy break up. It wasn't until he cheated on her, however, that she finally got the courage to leave him. Although it didn't end well, the relationship had allowed my mom an opportunity to grow. She grew in confidence as she found the courage to step away from an unhealthy situation, and she seemed to grow in hope too. She had hope now that she could go on without my dad. She would never forget him, she missed him daily, but life was here to be lived and she seemed determined to live it to the full.

I was trying to get on with my life too, taking it day-by-day. On the whole, college was tough for me. I was too afraid to raise my hand in class if I had a question for fear of getting teased or laughed at. To this day, I still have a fear of asking questions or talking in a large group. I know a lot of people have this fear, officially called "*glossophobia*", but I don't know if my fear is from being bullied over the years and losing my confidence, or if it is just the way I'm made.

After my dad died, I realized that being bullied was not the most horrible thing that could have happened to me. Losing my dad to suicide was. Having a parent die is horrible, but when a parent or loved one chooses suicide, it is not an accident. My dad decided to leave this earth and not be with us. If he had died from a natural cause such as a heart attack, or perhaps a car accident, it would have been more acceptable and understandable to me. I just didn't understand what I had done to deserve being bullied for all those years and then have to go through my dad's death.

During my college years I would meet new people and they would ask about my family. I would lie and tell them that my dad died from a heart attack. It was much easier to explain. I felt if any new people came into my life and found out the truth, they would judge me. Perhaps they would think I was somehow unstable myself. Also, I didn't want anyone to think my dad was a crazy man. He wasn't. Maybe I was trying to protect him. I think suicide was portrayed in the '90's and before as being the last option for people who were completely psycho. He was a normal human who was too hard on himself about the mistakes he had made. He was someone who was too proud to get the help he needed and obviously, he was depressed.

Although it was a difficult time, my college years showed me that there really can be life after being bullied and there is life after high school. I met so many wonderful people at college, people who had also had struggles at one point or another, and they too survived and had grown through their "storms". I also met and became friends with people from different races. Growing up in a small farm town, I had not had this opportunity. My understanding of people grew, my compassion for others grew, and most importantly, I slowly started to grow in confidence. I started to relax and not worry so much about my grades. I felt as though I could finally cut myself some slack. I still worried about talking in front of a large group of people, but bit-by-bit my confidence started to return.

> *"The tiny seed knew that in order to grow,*
> *it needed to be dropped in dirt, covered with darkness,*
> *and struggle to reach the light."*
>
> *Sandra Kring*

I remember one day during college having a revelation. It was as though I could suddenly see that I had my whole life stretched out ahead of me. The years during middle and high school were only a small portion of my life. I realized that there was a lot more life to be lived after school. I read somewhere once that the average life expectancy of females in the United States is around 81 years, and approximately 76 years for males. It made me think that, for a girl being bullied at the age of 10, it would be so comforting for her to know that she could still have over 70 years of life ahead of her. I so wished that I could make children and teens who are being bullied realize this!

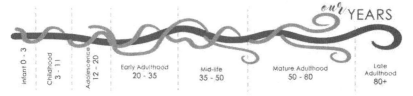

I wanted to be able to paste this timeline on the wall of every kid who is suffering at the hands of those who have no business making their lives as difficult as they are. I know it would have helped me to be able to look at it daily.

This was my season of growth. I felt somehow grounded, as though my strong roots were holding me firm, and allowing me the opportunity to slowly start stretching upwards. Just like a little seedling sending out its shoots towards the sun, I felt that I was also reaching towards the light.

"The purpose of life, after all, is to live it, to taste experience to the utmost, to reach out eagerly and without fear for newer and richer experience."
Eleanor Roosevelt

CHAPTER 8
love

Love
luv

Noun 1. a strong feeling of affection.
Synonyms: adoration, affection, reverence
"children fill their parents with feelings of love"
2. a great interest or pleasure in something
"you know how much I love ice-cream"
Verb 1. to feel deep affection for someone
Synonyms: esteem, respect, admire
"do you love me?"

I dated a couple of guys during my first and second year in college. I would occasionally compare the guys I dated to my dad. Maybe every young girl who had a good dad does that, or perhaps even if they had a not-so-nice one too? During my second year at SVSU I met a wonderful guy named Chris. We met while we were both working at Walmart to earn some extra money during those cash-strapped college years. He was going to the local community college while majoring in law enforcement. He was the most sincere and sensitive guy I had ever met. His family were equally amazing. I immediately loved the fact that he came from a great family with good morals, and who weren't afraid of hard work.

Chris had wavy dark brown hair, and small, bright blue eyes which reminded me of my dad's. He also wasn't very tall. Being short myself, I had always thought that it would just look plain weird if I ended up with a man who was over six feet tall! Chris was charming and had great integrity. I knew immediately that he was the kind of guy who would stand by someone if he believed in them and they were honest with him. He always had a good sense of character. He didn't grow up expecting to get the name brand clothes during his teen years. He worked while in high school and earned his own money, although he knew that his parents would always be there for him if he needed them. Chris and I got along so well. I felt like he "got" me.

During my second year at SVSU I had to decide on a major. I thought I wanted to study interior design but SVSU unfortunately does not offer that, so I had to transfer to another college in order to pursue my dream. I had taken the basic math, science, psychology and English classes that were required for transfer and so I did some research and discovered that Western Michigan University had a good interior design program.

I decided to transfer to WMU in the fall of 1995. My mom was sad that I was going to be three hours away from her. That first weekend, as I left her house to take the drive and start another chapter in my college years, she gave me a big hug and said "I love you". It was the first time I ever heard her say that. Since then, we have said it many times to each other and it feels good to say it and hear it. I always knew that she and my dad loved me, but unfortunately I didn't hear it.

After dating for just three months, Chris decided to move across the state with me while I attended WMU. He got a job working the third shift in a nearby manufacturing facility. He put off his college education after changing his mind about his major.

Although I was excited about this new chapter in my life, my insecurities and lack of confidence followed me to west Michigan. My thoughts about my dad and concern for my mom followed me too. I thought about my mom and worried about her often. Sometimes as I look back, I think I was running away from my problems, but they were following me.

I felt my mom didn't really have a secure shoulder to lean on with me so many miles away. My sister had her life with her new husband, and my brother was so busy with college and starting his career. Unfortunately, the close family connection we had once enjoyed on my dad's side wasn't close anymore. There were no big family holiday dinners or other family get-togethers anymore. I wondered if my dad's family blamed my mom for his death. Or did they blame my dad for his mom having a stroke and dying due to the stress? How come they weren't coming around to visit my mom anymore? My mom had so much guilt already as a result of my dad's death, I hated to think of her carrying this burden too. It was sad to know that she was largely on her own now, and so I tried to call her as often as I could, and I visited whenever my schedule allowed. Meanwhile, Chris and I broke up. I wanted to date others and have some freedom. I wanted to party, go dancing and drinking, and not think about anything. I wanted to forget all the bad memories from my past and just have fun. I wished that I could become a new person. I suppose that in some ways, I was rebelling. If someone could have given me a pill that enabled me to forget everything from 8th grade through to 12th grade, I would have taken it. A few months later, Chris took a job across the country in Arizona. He lived with his aunt and uncle. Although we had separated, I was secretly devastated by his move, and the fact that he could seemingly just go on without me. I continued going through the motions of going to school but my heart or mind weren't in it.

I enjoyed WMU, but I think the stress of college was getting to me. I enjoyed the classes I took in the interior design curriculum but felt that I wasn't focused enough. Just before my two years were up, I would have to present my portfolio in front of a team (which included the head of the program!) and they would decide if I got into the design program or not. They could only accept a small number of students each year into the program. If they didn't think my portfolio was good enough, I could try again the next year. I think I got nervous and my insecurities got the best of me. I didn't want to fail. I didn't know what I'd do if I didn't get accepted into the design program. I would feel embarrassed. I didn't want to hear it from the professionals that I wasn't good enough, so after a year and a half, I backed out and quit the program before anyone could tell me that I wouldn't make it.

Chris and I kept in touch while he was in Arizona. I thought of him often. The guys I would meet were nothing compared to Chris. We missed each other so much after five months of being apart that he asked if I would want to move out there to be with him permanently. Not knowing what direction my life was going in, and not sure what to do about college, I accepted his offer.

So on February 14, 1996, I drove to Indiana and Chris flew there to meet me. We drove across the country to start our life together once again. My Buick was packed from floor to ceiling with all my necessities while the rest were put in storage. In November of that same year, my brother and his buddy got my belongings out of storage and loaded up a U-Haul truck and drove to the house Chris and I had bought in Arizona. Things seemed to finally be falling in place for me. We were just so happy to be together.

Although life was settled, I still felt the need to go back to school. While working full time, I went back to college and gradually got my interior design degree at the community college near to where we lived. Chris also went back to college and got a degree in networking technologies. I was so proud of him. He still often says that if it weren't for me urging him on to go back to college, he probably never would have.

One summer day in 1999, Chris and I planned to go out to dinner. I assumed it was just to a local bar or restaurant, so I dressed casually in my black capris and leopard print blouse. While reaching in my closet to get my sandals, Chris wrinkled his nose at what I was wearing. He suggested I dress a little nicer. I felt a little insulted but went with the flow because I knew that he was never a fan of leopard print clothing. I changed into a cute dress and off we went. I asked him where we were going but he didn't really respond with a direct answer.

I became more and more curious, but also somewhat confused. Finally we arrived at Butte Mountain, and started the long drive up to the top. I had never been at the top so as we slowly made our way up the curved, narrow road, I was getting more excited. I felt happy that my boyfriend wasn't taking me to one of our usual places for dinner and was instead treating me to a surprise evening out. Once we got to the top of the mountain, we arrived at a really nice restaurant. An attendant approached our car and asked if we had reservations. I looked at Chris thinking, "Oh boy, now we'll need to turn around and go to another place." But Chris simply smiled at the attendant and said, "Yes, we do have reservations." At this point I began to feel just a little bit anxious!

Once inside the restaurant and finally seated, Chris ordered an expensive bottle of wine. I liked how he took control of the evening and planned it down to every detail. I remember feeling so loved and cherished. We ordered our food, and after our waiter left, Chris got off his chair. He came to my side of the table and got down on one knee and asked, "Will you marry me?"

I was surprised and so happy. He had finally proposed after being together for five years. I had dreamed of this moment over and over again, and it was finally here, and better than I could ever have imagined.

> *"You know you're in love when you can't fall asleep because reality is finally better than your dreams."*
>
>
> Dr. Seuss

We had a simply perfect evening together, and after leaving the restaurant, we began calling our families and telling them the good news. My mom was so excited for me. She had always had a soft spot for Chris and she knew that he made me happy. It delighted me to know that I was giving my mom a little bit of joy in the midst of her seemingly unending sadness. She was also a great asset when it came to planning our wedding, and this helped her to keep busy for a few months.

On June 17, 2000, Chris and I got married in Michigan. It was a beautiful, warm, sunny summer's day. It had been tough planning a wedding in Michigan while living in Arizona but with the help of my mom, mother-in-law and sister, we pulled it off. It was the happiest day of my life, and yet there was some sadness. I had never imagined that my brother would be the one walking me down the aisle, I had always thought it would be my dad.

As a little girl, I dreamed of my dad walking me down the aisle and handing me over to my future husband so we could say our vows. My dad would joke with my sister and me that he would "boot" us down the aisle whenever we got married, and gladly give us over to our future husbands. Oh how I wished he had been there to "boot" me down the aisle to Chris!

I would also imagine family pictures to be taken at the wedding with my new husband, with my parents on one side and his on the other. I was always proud that my parents were together, and that I didn't come from a split family as so many other Americans did. And yet, I was the one with the broken family now, not Chris.

We had about 200 guests at our wedding. There were double that amount invited to my sister's wedding eight years before ours. However, mom wanted to keep the count down since my dad wasn't around to assist financially and given that my brother had got married just one month earlier. I understood this and was so grateful to my mom for everything she did to make our day so special. It truly was a day I will never forgot, one filled with much happiness and love and laughter. I remember at one point wishing that I could somehow slow down time and make the day last longer! One of the highlights of my wedding day came while I was dancing with my new father-in-law and he said to me, "If I had to pick out someone to marry my son, it would be you." His beautiful and kind comment made me indescribably happy.

Chris and I went to Maui on our honeymoon. It was wonderful! We stayed at a beautiful resort on the Pacific Ocean. We went there without an agenda and planned our days as they approached. We rented a white convertible and drove around the island, shopping in little boutiques, art galleries and souvenir shops. We also went to our first luau which was a lot of fun. The luau consisted of belly dancers, music, a pig roast, comedians, great food and drinks. We even became quite adventurous and went parasailing and took a helicopter ride around the entire island. (The helicopter company bragged how they have never had an accident. One week after we took the ride, a helicopter from that same company crashed in the side of a mountain. We really counted our blessings when we heard this!) The weather in Maui was perfect for the entire ten days we were there. We felt so thankful that we could experience Maui before starting our life together as husband and wife. After the busyness of planning the wedding, it was a perfect time to relax together and have fun, not worrying about anything. As I did on our wedding day, I wished again that time would pause and we could enjoy these moments forever.

> "A successful marriage requires falling in love many times, always with the same person."
>
> *Mignon McLaughlin*

The honour of your presence is requested

at the marriage of

Brenda Jane

daughter of Ms. Charlotte Huber and

the late Gary Huber

to

Christopher Shawn Fitzmaurice

son of Mr. and Mrs. Joseph Fitzmaurice

on Saturday, the seventeenth of June

two thousand

at one-thirty in the afternoon

Chapel at Apple Mountain

4519 North River Road

Freeland, Michigan

Chris & I on our Wedding day

My brother, mom, myself, Chris & my sister
June 17, 2000

CHAPTER 9
home

Home
hōm

Noun 1. *the place where one lives permanently,
especially as a member of a family or household.*
Synonyms: *house, residence, habitat, dwelling, "this is our home"*
Verb 1. *the instinct of an animal to return to its territory after leaving it.*
"the birds were homing for their summer breeding grounds"
2. to move or be aimed towards with great accuracy.
Synonyms: *zero in, "the missiles homed in on the target"*

Chris and I had a lot of fun together during our first few years of marriage, although being married didn't feel very different to what we'd had before. I guess this was probably because we lived together before getting married. We enjoyed going out to eat, going to the local bar and listening to karaoke, watching movies together, going to ball games or concerts and just generally being in each other's company.

After a while though, we began to have some disagreements. Our arguments were mainly around the issue of children - I wanted to have kids but he wasn't ready for it just yet. We had discussed this prior to getting married but Chris had changed his mind and wanted to wait longer.

I had a lot of anxiety about money or lack thereof. Things were tight and we were constantly counting our pennies, so to speak. I got a design job after college working for a small "mom-pop" kitchen and bath company but I was only paid a commission. I am not a sales person, I am a designer and decorator. I wanted to be able to design and give the client a functional and aesthetically pleasing kitchen or bathroom. I had a hard time upselling something that was already functional.

Chris was having a hard time too and unfortunately started drinking. He had never been a big drinker before, but now he would drink alone on the weekend. He never drank during the work week but he would stay up late on Friday and Saturday nights, while I went to bed early, and would drink until the early hours of the morning. I would wake up to the sound of him crashing about as he eventually made his way to bed. I was always scared that he would do something to hurt himself and would hide his car keys under my pillow for fear of him taking off in his truck while he was drunk. I'm thankful this period of time didn't last long. I think Chris realized very soon that he could not act that way and put me through that distress any longer.

A few months later I got a job working for a larger company where I got paid a good hourly wage with benefits. I felt like a huge load had been lifted off of my shoulders and I'm sure off Chris' shoulders too. I began to feel less stressed. We were saving money and I loved my job. It's amazing how working for a good company and getting paid for what you believe you are worth can make a difference to your happiness. Maybe Chris noticed that and that's why he agreed to finally have a baby. We tried for about 18 months and then finally conceived in 2002.

I loved being pregnant even though I had morning sickness for the first three months. I loved going shopping and picking out baby items. I loved the attention people would give me as they noticed my big belly. I loved feeling my baby kick and move around in my tummy. The baby got the hiccups quite often which would shake my belly and would make me laugh. Every day, I was so amazed that there was actually a little person inside my belly - a real live person!

I had an ultra sound done and we wanted to find out the sex of our baby. I'm a "planner" so knowing the sex enabled me to start buying clothes and start decorating the baby's room. When I left my doctor's appointment after finding out I was having a girl, I immediately called Chris from the car. I was so excited that I drove through a red light in a large, usually busy intersection. The intersection had on and off ramps to the interstate. As I was half way through I realized that I had just run the red light. I panicked and looked around but there were no cars to be seen. I know God must have had my back, I still go cold thinking about what could have gone wrong.

One Sunday evening while eating supper, my water broke. I called the doctor and we drove to the hospital. Our little girl, Kailyn Jane, was born on March 24, 2003. She was a month early, but was healthy. Chris and my friend Rebecca were in the delivery room with me. Chris was able to stay by my side throughout the entire delivery without fainting. Delivery wasn't as scary as I expected it to be. The nurses were wonderful and my friend was helpful in trying to make me feel relaxed. I think Chris didn't really know what to do but this was new to both of us. The moment Kailyn was born was one of the happiest of my life. Chris got a bit of a fright at first though, when Kailyn appeared. He thought she had a tail on her little behind, but luckily it was only a little turd! We've laughed about his shocked reaction many times since. We were both in awe of this little miracle, our baby girl was perfect!

Having Kailyn was the most wonderful feeling ever! I could not believe I was finally a mom. She was so precious and tiny. I felt that I could stare at her all day long and never get bored. I could not believe that Chris and I had made this little creature. I would smile when I'd see Chris smiling and staring at our little one with such love, pride and adoration. However, I felt again saddened to know that my dad would never be able to hold her and love her as her other grandparents were able to.

Chris and I discussed moving back to Michigan to be closer to our family since we had started a family of our own. Family is very important to me. I wanted my child to grow up around her grandparents, aunts and uncles and cousins, just as I had done. Eventually Chris and I decided to start looking for jobs in Michigan. In November of 2003, I got a job near Detroit and drove back to Michigan to start work. My mom flew out to Arizona so she could ride back east with Kailyn and me. Chris stayed behind in Arizona to sell the house and pack up. Our house sold quickly (within four days) and once we closed on it, Chris loaded up the U-Haul truck along with our dog, Ladie, and drove back to Michigan to be with us.

I soon learned though that the design job I had accepted wasn't what I expected. The company I was working for had huge financial problems. My paychecks were bouncing. Week after week, as I tried to cash my paycheck, it would bounce. I was devastated to think that I had packed up my family, driven 2200 miles and started a new job, for *this*!

One day, I attended a design seminar hosted by one of the cabinet vendors whom we did business with. There I met a lady who was looking for design help for her company. This company was located only a few miles from my mom's house. I set a day aside, went for the interview and got the job. For a few months, we lived with my mom. Chris started his search for a job. He wasn't one to sit around and not work, and of course financially we couldn't have him out of work for too long. He finally got an offer and started his new job in March 2004. We felt our lives would be back to normal as soon as we found a house of our own.

It didn't take long before we closed on a newly built house in the country, 20 miles from my mom's house. It was situated in between my job and Chris' new job. It felt good to be living back in the country where there are open fields, trees and no stop lights. We had enjoyed the big city and night life in Arizona, but there is something about the peacefulness and safe feeling the country has to offer. I love that saying, "You can take the girl out of the country, but you can't take the country out of the girl." I had to go back to my country roots. Merrill was our new home. It was a great little town where we could get to know the people and get involved in the community.

Only a few months into my new job, I got news from my boss that my full-time job with benefits was to be downscaled to a part time position with no benefits. I could not believe what I was hearing. The economy was taking a down turn and I didn't know what I would do. I was paying full-time daycare prices so now I had to find a part time daycare for Kailyn. It was a really difficult time for me. I had to juggle my job and, at the same time, search for a local daycare and someone who I felt was qualified to care for my precious little daughter. Unfortunately, my boss did not agree with me spending time during the day to search for a new daycare. One day she demanded that I just select any daycare and be done with it. In what was perhaps a very rash decision, I quit my job on the spot. I did not want to be rushed into finding a new daycare without getting references and interviewing the prospects. I called Chris first to ask his advice and permission. He agreed with me. Our little girl was to take priority over any job.

I was devastated. I thought I had finally gotten on a steady career path at this company. I didn't know what to do as I packed up the few things I had in the office. I cried while driving the 20 minutes back home. I thought I had my husband's support in the decision we made together, but as soon as I got home, the first thing he said to me was, "You need to find a job."

I knew I needed to work but I was a wreck. I hated the thought of leaving our daughter with a stranger. I started to think that perhaps I was not meant to be a designer. I had had four design jobs within the last few years and three of them had turned sour. Maybe we shouldn't have left Arizona where I loved my job? I felt that I was to blame for leaving Arizona. After all, I was the one who initiated the move.

Once again, I felt lost and worthless. I went into a deep depression and had to knock it out of myself. I knew that I had to pick myself up and be strong for our daughter. One night at around 3 a.m., I woke up suddenly. I started crying and thinking about my life. I felt I hadn't accomplished anything and I felt like a loser. While Chris was sleeping, I went into the bathroom and shut the door to not waken him. I laid on the floor and cried. I felt myself going into a deep, dark place that really scared me. I imagined that this was how my dad must have felt. I briefly thought, "If only I had a gun."

I didn't know what direction to go in or who to turn to. I felt that I wasn't getting any support from my husband and I knew that I couldn't burden my mom with my problems. I had no true friends nearby. I had to start thinking about my baby in the next room and I knew that I needed to survive for her. I really wanted it to end though. I wanted the stress and uneasiness to end. I wanted to be happy again. I wanted to belong and feel as though I was accomplishing something with my life. I knew what my dad's suicide had done to me and my family though, and so I picked myself up off the floor, determined to carry on. I went back to bed and cried myself to sleep.

I had to come up with a plan, something positive to focus on. I needed to have a goal and something to look forward to. I thought about selling real estate. My sister knew someone in the area who was a realtor so she got some information for me and I started taking real estate classes. I passed the state exam with flying colors and became an accredited realtor. My mom agreed to babysit Kailyn off and on since I had a flexible schedule. I could even take Kailyn with me to show a house if I got in a bind. I enjoyed the flexibility of it and I enjoyed showing houses. The interior design side of me could see potential in almost every house I entered. Unfortunately, not all buyers could see that. I found that I was spending more than I was making between all the advertising fees I had to pay, my continuing education, mileage and daily gas. I knew eventually that it wasn't a long-term career option for me. In addition to my costs, the housing market was crashing and it was a bad time to get into the real estate business. Even the realtors who had been in the business for a while were struggling. Again, I felt that I had started something I couldn't finish and I was defeated after just two and a half years of trying.

I did have some fulfilling moments while selling real estate. It was a great feeling when a young couple closed on their first house. The looks on their faces were well worth everything. Another client, a retired veteran named Howard, was a divorced African-American Christian. I helped him find a beautiful place he could call home. He and I struck up a friendship and we would meet with our Bibles at the local Tim Horton's for a bite to eat and talk about our faith. We would discuss how the Bible related to everyday life. I would talk about the struggles I had had in the past, about being bullied and about my dad's suicide. I discussed my career path with him too. We prayed together many times and got to know each other well. When I told him about my experience of the hand coming through my window the first night after my dad's death, he was the one who believed that it was God's hand. I thought that maybe it was my dad's hand comforting me, but when Howard explained it, it made more sense to me that it was God's hand.

I think my meetings with Howard were the turning point of really wanting to find a church to belong to. I wanted to get to know the Bible stories and I wanted my daughter to grow up knowing God. I wanted her to know that it's wonderful and comforting to pray. Growing up in the Lutheran church, I felt I was forced to go to church because that's what my dad did and we were expected to follow. I wasn't interested in the stories of the Bible when I was younger. It was as if I didn't understand the purpose of the stories or how they relate to everyday life. I didn't understand that Jesus, during his time on earth, experienced all the same emotions that I had experienced in my life so far. I yearned to learn more about God and be a part of something bigger than my daily routine of going to work, coming home and taking care of a family.

I introduced Howard to my mom and they would discuss the Bible too. I was feeling more optimistic about life and I figured that maybe my mom could benefit from hearing about God's word too. Howard hoped to be a positive influence on my mom, he wanted to bring some light and happiness into her world again. They would meet once in a while for lunch and just talk like he and I did.

Unfortunately, after a few months, Howard started to change and act strangely. He started becoming bossy and aggressive. He even told my mom that he was going to marry me someday. I think he was falling in love with me, but I also believe that there was an element of mental illness in his life that I hadn't noticed before. I was deeply saddened by this. The trust I had for him was shattered. The one positive thing that came out of meeting him was that he brought me closer to Jesus and taught me so much about the Bible. I felt let down though, I had trusted Howard so much and even introduced him to my mom. How could God allow this man to do something so good as spreading the message of the Bible, and yet allow him to disappoint us so much? I guess God uses all types, and sometimes we just don't understand his ways. I took comfort from the words in Isaiah 55, verse 8 and 9, which say:

> "For my thoughts are not your thoughts,
> neither are your ways my ways,"
> declares the LORD.
> "As the heavens are higher than the earth,
> so are my ways higher than your ways
> and my thoughts than your thoughts[5]."

While I didn't always understand His ways, I was learning that that was ok. It was ok to trust God with what was happening in my life - the good and the bad.

I really did miss the design industry and so I soon started looking for another design job. I found one at a small family-owned business. The owner was a wonderful Christian man. I loved my job there. I ran the showroom and designed kitchens and bathrooms. I even dreamed that maybe one day I could take over when he retired. After the rollercoaster of ups and downs we'd be through, things seemed to be going so well. Chris and I were getting along great and saving money. We were really happy.

However, as had happened so often before, my dream came to an end quickly. Sadly my boss had to let me go due to finances and the fact that he had to close down his shop. It felt like yet another heartbreak in my life. I immediately applied for unemployment benefits, but within two weeks I had found a new job. Another small company contacted me after they learned about the shop closing. Although it was only a part-time job, it was better than no job at all and so I accepted the position. I still felt so frustrated though, and somehow incomplete. When was my career going to finally get off the ground? When would I feel that I had a purpose, and could do something to help others?

One rainy Friday afternoon I let our dog, Ladie, outside to do her business. When I finally remembered that she was outside, she was nowhere to be seen. We went outside and yelled her name, and eventually we drove around the area. We assumed that she couldn't have gone far with those short Basset Hound legs of hers. She was a mixed breed of Basset Hound and black Labrador. Her body was that of a hound but she had the head of a lab. She was a great dog with a mellow personality and was great around our newborn.

Friday evening came and we were really worried. I imagined that Ladie would be cold and hungry. On Saturday we still couldn't find her. We thought she was lost forever. I was devastated. She was our "baby" before we had a baby. While eating dinner on Sunday, we got a knock at the door. There was a lady standing there who introduced herself as Christine and asked if we had lost a dog. She had found our Ladie! She said Ladie had been outside the church around the corner from our house all weekend. She had seen her there while she attended an event on Saturday and had assumed it was a neighbor's dog. But while walking into church on Sunday, she had noticed the same dog. She had told her husband that if the dog was still in the parking lot after the service, they were going to take her home. Of course, Ladie stuck around after the Sunday service and got a ride with the family back to their house. They fed her and were surprised to notice that Ladie had a dog tag from Arizona. Christine called the Arizona animal humane society. They would not give her our names but did tell her that the dog's name was Ladie. After talking to the pastor at church, she found out that we were from Arizona because the week we moved in, that pastor knocked on our door to welcome us to the area. We thanked Christine and her family for bringing Ladie back home. I was so grateful for all the trouble she'd gone to in order to locate us. Before leaving, Christine invited us to join them at their church around the corner on the following Sunday.

Chris, Kailyn, Ladie and I

During the difficult few months of not knowing what direction my career would take me, I had found myself praying more and more. I prayed about finding the right job, but I also found myself praying about finding the right church to attend. I had talked to Chris about finding a church to join so that Kailyn would know what it was like to have a church family and to be able to go to Sunday school. Chris, at the time, had no desire to attend church, but I took Christine up on her offer. Kailyn and I attended the church around the corner on our own. I felt really nervous walking into a church by myself with my baby. I was nervous about where I would sit and what I would do if Kailyn got cranky. I looked for Christine and her family and sat with them. The people at Merrill Wesleyan Church welcomed us with open arms.

I later attended a class to learn more about the background of the Wesleyans since I had only ever known about the Lutheran denomination. I soon realized that

Wesleyanism wasn't very different to the Lutheran beliefs. Maybe a little more singing and praising the Lord during the service, but our Bibles were the same and we basically had the same beliefs.

During the class I attended, I met a sweet lady named Debbie. Since I was only working part time, I had time during the week to take a private Bible class with her at her house. It worked out well and I really enjoyed it. I learned so much from her. I told her about my past and she prayed with me. She tried to help me forgive my dad and let go of the anger I had towards him for what he did. I also confided in her that I really did need to get a full-time job, but that I had no idea what I wanted to do with the rest of my life. I felt I didn't have the ability to make a difference. I wanted to make a difference in my life and in the lives of others I encountered. Debbie's husband was the CFO of a large local hospital. She asked him to see if there was anything he could do for me. I only had design experience and some office and purchasing experience so I didn't let myself get my hopes up when she told me about her conversation with her husband.

The next time we met Debbie told me to email my resume to her husband. He had told her that there was a position about to open up in accounts payable due to a lady moving out of state. I sent him my resume and got an interview. I was over the moon when I heard that I got the job! It was full time with benefits. Around the time of the interview, I had just discovered that I was pregnant again. I was so excited. A new job and a new baby! Perhaps, I thought, this is the career path I'm supposed to take. It felt so right, like this was the route God was taking me on. Apparently I was not destined to work in the design industry after all.

Three days after starting my job at the hospital, I dropped Kailyn off at day care and was about two miles from our house. I saw a police car up ahead and a wrecked vehicle on the side of the road. It was very early in the morning so it was still dark. I slowly drove up to the accident scene, headed in an easterly direction. I saw a jeep facing west. I suddenly panicked, thinking it might be Chris' jeep, but then thought that it couldn't be his jeep because he would also be travelling east to work. As I looked closer, I saw that it was a white jeep Cherokee, the exact same vehicle my husband drove. I started to shake and pray out loud, "Oh please, Lord, let him be ok!"

I slowly rolled down my window and told the officer, who was directing traffic, that I thought it was my husband's jeep. He told me that the ambulance had already taken him to Covenant Hospital and that he was conscious, or that's what I thought he said. I later found out that he actually said "unconscious." I'm glad I heard "conscious" instead because I would have been even more distraught if I had heard him correctly. I called my mom immediately and told her about the accident and asked her to call Chris' parents.

I only knew how to get to Covenant Hospital in the downtown area because I had had to go for exams recently. That is where our baby was going to be delivered and I was due in just over three months. Then I called Chris' boss, to make them aware of the accident and finally I called my boss. I was shaking all the way to the hospital and found myself in a downward spiral of negative thoughts, "What if Chris isn't alright and I have to raise two little girls on my own? How will I cope without him?"

I made it to the hospital and entered the ER waiting room. The lady behind the counter said that Chris was getting a CAT scan and would be done shortly. A few minutes later, I was able to go to the room to see my husband. He was conscious and was able to talk to me. The last thing he remembered was kissing me good-bye and walking out the door. It was October 1, the first day of bow season and he was so excited to be able to leave work early that day to go up north and possibly shoot a buck. He ended up staying one night in the hospital. His body was sore all over when he came home and he was off of work for a few days. Unfortunately he missed bow season that year.

I'm thankful Chris got a hobby since moving back to Michigan. He loves hunting and fishing. He hadn't done any of those things while we were in Arizona. He also took up recreational shooting and bought himself a pistol. He tried to convince me to get one and said that shooting could be an activity we could do together. I was very hesitant about learning to shoot a gun. The worrier in me feared that if I ever got into a dark, dark place again, would I want to take my own life? It would be too easy to load the pistol, shoot and end everything quickly. I know there are many other ways to end your life, but I feel shooting yourself could be done too quickly and easily if you knew how to load a pistol and handle one. Plus, there would be no turning back after you attempted it. I just didn't want to go down that road and so I left Chris to enjoy his shooting on his own.

I had another easy pregnancy and, once again, really enjoyed the experience. However, a week before Christmas I was put on strict bed rest due to early contractions. During this time, the families in our church were wonderful. They brought Chris and me meals so he didn't have to cook. I had never known of a church like this. I didn't even know the names of some of the people who brought us food. Chris was wonderful too. He took great care of me and made sure I didn't do anything I wasn't supposed to do.

Our second little girl, Reagan Grace, was finally born on January 6, 2009. She was so perfect and we were overjoyed that Kailyn had a little sister. It felt good to be a family of four.

When Reagan was just a week old I received a call from the hospital where she was born to say that we needed to go to the Lansing hospital to get her tested for Cystic Fibrosis.

Apparently, on the day she was born, she had tested positive for it. This was a fairly new test the hospitals gave babies. I was in shock. I had no idea that she'd even undergone the test, let alone received a result like this. I immediately looked up information about Cystic Fibrosis as I knew nothing about it, and the lady who called me wasn't very forthcoming in answering my questions. According to the Cystic Fibrosis Foundation, "this progressive genetic disease causes persistent lung infections and limits the ability to breathe over time. A defective gene causes a thick, sticky buildup of mucus in the lungs, pancreas, and other organs. In the lungs, the mucus clogs the airways and traps bacteria leading to infections, extensive lung damage, and eventually, respiratory failure. In the pancreas, the mucus prevents the release of digestive enzymes that allow the body to break down food and absorb vital nutrients[6]".

I couldn't believe the bad news. It couldn't be happening to us. I called Chris at work crying so much that he could barely make head or tail of what I was trying to tell him. He was also shocked. I scheduled our appointment down in Lansing for two weeks later. In the meantime, I let my church family know about our news so that they could pray for us. It gave me so much comfort knowing that I could reach out for help like this. I was a nervous wreck on the day that we took our baby girl to Lansing. There was a sweat test the nurses had to do on her. They wrapped her tiny arms in plastic to do the test. We got the results the same day. The numbers that came back were not clear and the test was said to be inconclusive. Reagan's results fell into somewhat of a "gray area" and this meant that we had to make yet another appointment and go back two weeks later. She had another sweat test but this time we were unable to find out the results on the same day.

The waiting game really got to me. It was all I could think about the entire time I was on maternity leave. I tried to pray and ask God for peace, but it was so hard not knowing whether Reagan was sick or not. She seemed so healthy to me. Finally, we received a call saying that Reagan did not have cystic fibrosis, she was just a carrier of it. People with CF have inherited two copies of the defective CF gene, one copy from each parent. People with only one copy of the defective CF gene are called carriers, but they do not have the disease. Over the years, more studies have been done to help the lives of the people with Cystic Fibrosis. In the 1960's and 1970's, people with CF were only expected to live until their teenage years but now most sufferers live well into their thirties. I thanked God all day after hearing the good news, it was such a relief.

I still believe that the wonderful news had to do with all the prayers my church family said for us. From the time I got that first call to the time we received the final results, I worried about what was going to happen to our little girl. The statistics were not in our favor. The life expectancy of people with Cystic Fibrosis was increasing year after year, but she would not lead a "normal" life. We would have been running her to the hospital every time she caught a little cold. I have such compassion for people suffering with CF, and for those who have family members with it. I am hopeful with all the research that is being done that a cure will be found soon!

I think after being on bed rest and Reagan's diagnosis, Chris realized that our church played a big role in getting us through it. Chris started attending church with me and our girls. I had prayed that he would. Chris admitted to me that we seemed to get along and treat each other better when we went to church regularly. Going to church makes me want to be a better person. It gives me reassurance that no matter what happens, God will be there and get me through it. I enjoy going to church. Many times, I feel as though our pastor is talking only to me and knows of any struggles I had the prior week or will have in the week to come.

It felt so good to finally be home. Yes, I had come home to Michigan, but in another way I felt like I had come home to this church family. Finding a community of believers to join had been like a home-coming of a spiritual kind. I knew that this was where I was meant to be.

Chris, Kailyn, Reagan and I

"The magic thing about home is that it feels good to leave, and it feels even better to come back."
Anonymous

CHAPTER 10

FINDING answers

Answer

ansər

Noun 1. *a thing that is said, written or done as a reaction to a question, statement or situation.*
Synonyms: *reply, response, return, reaction*
"I opened the door without waiting for an answer"
2. *a solution to a problem or dilemma.*
Synonyms: *solution, remedy, quick fix*
"having more money is not the answer"
Verb 1. *to say or write something as a reaction to someone or something. "Yes, I can see you," she answered.*
2. *to act in reaction to. "he answered the phone"*

After having Reagan, I started thinking about my dad more often and, in particular, the moments he was missing out on. Now I had two daughters who my dad would never see or hold. They would never see their grandpa or get to sit on his lap, hear his voice and get to know him personally. I would tell my girls about their grandpa, his love for farming and how he used to tease me. I hope that through my stories, his memory is kept alive. I prayed often that my dad made it to heaven. My mom was getting older but she truly still missed him. I know she hopes to one day be with him in heaven when it is her time to go.

I had so many questions. Was my dad in heaven? Was

suicide a sin?

A few years ago, after spending much time worrying about it, I talked to my pastor about my dad and asked him if he thought my dad went to heaven even though he took his own life. My pastor's response was, "Taking your own life is a sin."

Although I respected my pastor very much, his answer left an uneasy feeling in the pit of my stomach. I would pray about it at night and sometimes as I was driving to work. For some reason, I couldn't stop thinking about it. I wanted God to give me a sign of some sort that my dad had made it to heaven. My dad was a good man who made one big mistake. Had God forgiven him and allowed him into heaven for eternity?

One day while I was working, Jill, a lady I had met from another department in the hospital, came by my desk. We had discovered a few months before that her cousin had married my cousin. Boy, it really is a small world! Jill handed me an article and said to read it. I read the title. It said, "God has special affection for suicide victims". I will never forget the shivers I felt running up and down my arms. I asked her, "How did you know?"

She looked at me strangely. I told her briefly about my dad and how I'd been praying that God would somehow let me know that my dad was in heaven.

For some unknown reason, after she had read the article at home, she decided to bring it into the office and show me. I felt like I finally had my answer in black and white. The article was written by Father Ron Rolheiser[7]. He stated that a suicide victim is unhealthy, and suicide is a disease, "the emotional equivalent to cancer". Nobody who is emotionally healthy really wants to die or put their family and loved ones through the pain that will be caused by their death. The illness takes a person out of life against his or her will. He proceeded to say that it's the humble people who commit suicide, not the insensitive ones. That was truly my dad.

Father Ron reassured his readers that victims are inside God's embrace enjoying freedom they could not enjoy here on earth. He went on to say that God judges each of us on our entire Christian life, rather than upon a single mistake. The Bible states in Romans 8:38, "And I am convinced that nothing can ever separate us from God's love. Neither death nor life, neither angels nor demons, neither our fears for today nor our worries about tomorrow - not even the powers of hell can separate us from God's love[8]."

I know now that God's love can reach into the darkest of places and rescue a wounded soul. It rescued me. I also know that God's love can reach the most unlovable soul, and if we are willing to accept it, He offers us the gift of a place in eternity with Him. God has a way of turning any pain around for good and can use it to strengthen us and, through us, to help others. We all die with sins not named or repented of, but God knows. Is one sin, such as suicide, worse than another? The Bible states that all of us have sinned[9], we all fall short of how God would want us to be. I like to think that perhaps that was what my pastor was referring to. However, he neglected to tell me about God's loving embrace and that one sin does not need to determine whether we spend eternity in heaven or not.

I felt as if a load had been taken off my shoulders after I'd read the article by Father Ron. My prayers were answered. It's easy to stop praying too soon and carry all the burden on your own. Jesus makes it clear in Matthew 11:28, where He said, "Come to me, all of you who are weary and carry heavy burdens, and I will give you rest[10]."

I later read a book called *When God Winks*: How the Power of Coincidence Guides Your Life by Squire Rushnell. A "God wink" is an event or personal experience that can be seen as a sign of divine intervention, often perceived as an answer to a prayer. Some people call it a coincidence.

Receiving the article from Jill was truly a "God wink" moment and I don't believe it was just coincidence that she decided to show it to me. She could have shown any one of the six ladies near my desk but she chose me. God used my co-worker as His messenger to get me the answer I had been seeking. The glorious answer that my dad is with Him, free of pain. That is awesome!

I always questioned why I got the job at the hospital. Wasn't there someone more qualified than I was? I was a fast learner but I wasn't an accountant or a business major. I went with the flow of things but I still felt somehow out of place there. However, I now believe that God put me there for a reason. Maybe it was just to meet Jill and to ultimately find the answers to my questions about my dad going to heaven? Or perhaps it was to make me feel content financially and lead me to the next chapter in my life? Maybe it was both?

A few months after having Reagan, I began having some throat issues. It felt as if my throat was constantly burning. I contacted my doctor and he thought it was acid reflux. He prescribed me a variety of medicines but nothing worked. He then thought that it might be a hiatal hernia caused from labor. A hiatal hernia occurs when part of your stomach pushes upward through your diaphragm. Your diaphragm normally has a small opening through which your esophagus passes on its way to connect to your stomach. The stomach can push up through this opening and cause a hiatal hernia. A large hiatal hernia can allow food and acid to reflux into the esophagus, which in my case would cause a burning throat.

When my symptoms didn't improve, my doctor eventually referred me to a Gastroenterologist. I had an upper endoscopy done and the doctor discovered that I did not have a hiatal hernia but instead that I had celiac disease. According to the Celiac Disease Foundation, "celiac disease is a serious autoimmune disorder that can occur in genetically predisposed people where the ingestion of gluten (protein found in wheat, rye and barley) leads to damage in the small intestine. It is estimated to affect 1 in 100 people worldwide[11]." Two and a half million Americans are undiagnosed and are at risk for long-term health complications. The only symptoms I had were joint pain in my right hand and a "full" feeling in my stomach when I ate at times. I just thought that I was eating too much and so I started having smaller portions and, as a result, started losing weight. Little did I know the damage that was being done to my small intestines over the years. As a result of eating gluten the villi, which are the tiny, hair-like structures found on the lining of the small intestines, were being flattened. They should stand up straight, like the fibers on a plush carpet. If people suffering from celiac disease continue to eat gluten, eventually they become malnourished as the body is no longer able to absorb the nutrients from food. I also eventually found out that my burning throat thankfully had nothing to do with having celiac disease and instead all I needed was some cortisone nose spray.

Living with celiac disease was a struggle. I recall hearing about my cousin's two little boys having the condition and saying to Chris, "I couldn't imagine living with a disease like that one. I enjoy eating anything and everything."

But I am living with it now and it has been life changing for me. For over thirty years I could eat what I wanted, but once I was diagnosed I had to start reading labels and questioning the waitresses and menus in restaurants. Research shows that celiac disease is hereditary and can cause depression and many other symptoms. Maybe my dad had it but was never aware? However, we ate so healthily living on our farm and off the land, that we actually ate very little gluten at all.

I didn't want to believe that I had celiac disease so I decided to get a second opinion at the University of

Michigan. They confirmed that I did have the disease. I didn't believe I had it because I didn't associate the symptoms I had with anything unusual. I was told that I had most likely had it my whole life and that various events could have triggered it. I thought that I would have been diagnosed with it years ago after dealing with the tragedy of Dad's death. However, a number of other events could apparently have triggered the disease instead, including my pregnancy with Reagan.

I started to read a book my mother-in-law bought me called *The G Free Diet* by Elisabeth Hasselbeck. It's about the author's struggle with celiac disease and being misdiagnosed for years. I had the book with me on my desk at work one day when my friend Diana noticed it. I had gotten to know Diana quite well while working at the hospital. She inquired about the book and I told her I was recently diagnosed with celiac disease. I told her of the symptoms that a person could experience with the disease and she said, "I think I have it too. The symptoms you mentioned describe what I've been dealing with for the past 10 years."

She asked to borrow the book when I was finished with it. After she read what foods to eat and which ones to stay away from, she started following the recommendations and felt like an entirely new person.

Perhaps this was another "God wink" experience? I had been questioning my role in this job and through experiences like the ones I had with Jill and Diana, it seemed as though I was finding answers. Perhaps God's purpose for placing me in my role at the hospital was for Diana to regain control of her health and for me to find peace about my dad's place in heaven.

Since being diagnosed with celiac disease nine years ago, I feel as if I should help others who have it in any way I can. I did not receive much guidance from anyone when I was diagnosed. I had to research the types and brands of food that were gluten free. It was very frustrating for me. Just when I thought I found a product that was gluten free, the manufacturer would change the ingredients, and it would no longer be gluten free. Fortunately, grocery stores and restaurants have come a long way in providing a larger selection of gluten free foods. However, the cost of these items is still about double compared to non-gluten free alternatives.

Whenever I'm in the gluten free aisle at the grocery store, and another shopper is also nearby shopping for gluten free food, I feel compelled to start a conversation with him or her, and to share information like recipes or ideas for meals. Living with celiac is a learning curve for everyone and from my experience, I feel it's helpful talking to others who are going through the same thing. Recently I started chatting with a lady who was looking in the gluten free section and she shared that her granddaughter had recently been diagnosed. I shared some helpful tips pertaining to a couple of gluten free recipes and she was really appreciative. Unfortunately, in my experience of talking to doctors about eating gluten free, they make it seem as if it's no big deal. It is a big deal though because your entire lifestyle has to change. I challenged one doctor to try to eat gluten free for a month. She didn't ever take me up on the challenge though.

After working at the hospital for two and a half years, I found out that my job would be moving to another state. Once again I had to start looking for a new job. My time in the hospital finance department had helped me to find so many of the answers I was looking for. Although I could not believe that I was in the job market yet again, I was so grateful for the many good days I had there and for the wonderful people I had met. It left me with a slightly panicked feeling though, knowing that I was now in my thirties and did not have a stable career yet. When I was younger, this is not what I imagined my life would be like. I imagined living in a big city and working for a large design firm in an extravagant office. However, living in Arizona, I realized that I didn't want to raise my girls in the big city. I wanted to raise them in the country and give them similar roots to my own. However, I thought I'd at least be working for a design firm doing what I was passionate about!

Soon after I found out I was losing my job at the hospital, Chris noticed that the tax and accounting firm he worked for was hiring a part-time administrative staff member. I questioned the opportunity though since it was only part-time and we really needed the full-time income. He suggested that maybe I could get my own design business going on the side. I was doing a little decorating here and there for a few people during that time anyway. He could see the passion I had for it. I applied for the administrative position and was offered the job. I accepted it and was quite happy about my decision. After working there for only four months, I got offered another position which was full-time. Chris and I were excited. We didn't have any concerns about working for the same firm. Our paths wouldn't cross often since his office was on the first floor and mine on the second.

I would be working in the finance department and processing payables just as I had done in my previous job. Sometimes I think God has a great sense of humor! I always used to say that I hated working with numbers and could never do it. I have since found out that I enjoy working with numbers and spreadsheets. I've learned to *never* say never!

I felt that I *finally* had job security and I hoped that the bad luck I'd had in the previous companies I'd worked for wouldn't follow me to my new position. Maybe I was a little superstitious though. I didn't want to "jinx" this firm and have Chris and I both out of a job! I knew that I couldn't think like that though. I mean, what are the chances?

Having no formal training in accounting, I felt the need to get an accounting degree. I applied at the local community college and took an accounting class which I enjoyed, and also continued to take economics and statistics. I did really well but found that I was quickly getting stressed and overwhelmed. I felt I had no time for my family. I worked during the day, had classes two evenings a week and studied on the weekend. I finally made the decision to quit college and try to be content with my full-time job, so I could spend more time with my family. I realized how my kids were growing up too fast and I didn't want to miss that. I finally understood what I had heard older people say to me so often, "Enjoy your kids while they are young because they will grow up fast. Time goes faster when you have kids of your own."

During my time at the accounting firm, I have been able to do a little decorating here and there. I decorated the lobby area, along with the second floor office spaces. Decorating spaces and making them look beautiful fills a void in me. It is such a natural high to do what I love. I've discovered that I don't feel overwhelmed when I am busy doing what I enjoy. Maybe this is true for all of us? Perhaps our insecurities about not being able to do something properly cause us to feel overwhelmed and anxious? I think that maybe I was afraid to fail at getting my accounting degree.

As I look back now, I am amazed by how things have fallen into place. At times I believed that I knew what was best for my life (don't we all, at one stage or another?), but as I've examined the way that many things have turned out, I've found that God really does know what He's doing and, more than that, He knows just how much I can manage. I believe God knew that I could only handle two children who are six years apart in age. I get easily flustered and stressed, if I had had more babies, I don't think I could have done as good a job as I've managed to do with my girls. I also often worry about our finances. God knew I needed to feel as though I was contributing equally to our income. He provided me with a good job where I can happily say that I have a career.

Through the years and many experiences that I've had, both the good and the bad, I've learned that sometimes the answers to my questions don't come immediately. But they do come. As long as we're prepared to look for the answers to our questions, God promises to show up for us. Sometimes these moments are small, little "winks" from the One who knows us better than we know ourselves.

> *"Don't dwell on what went wrong,*
> *instead focus on what to do next.*
> *Spend your energies on moving forward*
> *toward finding the answer."*
> *Denis Waitley*

CHAPTER 11

Season
sēzən

Noun 1. each of the four divisions of the year (spring, summer, autumn, and winter) marked by particular weather patterns and daylight hours, resulting from the earth's changing position with regard to the sun.
Verb 1. to add salt, herbs, pepper, or other spices to (food).
Synonyms: flavor, spice
"season the meat with salt and pepper" 2. to make wood suitable for use as timber by adjusting its moisture content to that of the environment in which it will be used.
Synonyms: mature, age, mellow, condition, acclimatize, prepare, prime, ripen

We all know what seasons are. Living in Michigan, one cannot escape the seasons and the changing scenes as time marches on each year. I love summer in Michigan, which for our family usually means going to the beach, floating around on our boat, bike riding and hanging out by the campfire in the evenings. Summer means warmth and light and freedom and ice-cream! Then, unfortunately, the warmth of summer gradually ends as the evenings get chillier and the days get shorter. Autumn makes its appearance although it isn't always so bad. Autumn brings the beautiful warm colors of reds, oranges and yellows. It's a time to start slowing down. Maybe the thought of summer leaving doesn't have to be so sad, with the many autumn colors still available to see and admire.

After autumn, winter usually appears with a roar. The days are short and cold. I tend to stay indoors, read a book and watch movies in my spare time. Even though I feel a little glum during these months, I need to remind myself that now is the time to reflect and appreciate the things we have and the people who are in our lives. Although winter means cold and darkness and barren landscapes, it also means fire-side conversations, warm blankets and Christmas.

After winter, I really look forward to spring. The ground thaws, flowers start to bloom and the leaves on the trees return. I'm generally in a better mood when spring comes around! Spring brings growth, newness and refreshing.

Seasons are important. Each one is different, but each one is necessary. Although I've never particularly loved winter, I realize the need for it, and I recognize the unique beauty of it too. What could be more beautiful than the Michigan countryside after a fresh snowfall? Seasons also help to mark the passage of time. My dad left us in the spring, and each year spring provides me with a chance to remember that another year has gone by.

I first heard about the different times in our lives being referred to as "seasons" by my friend Joy, and then my pastor mentioned it in one of his sermons. It seemed so fitting to me and such a wonderful analogy of how life works. It also explained so much about the relationships we have with others. People can come into our lives during one season, but then the season will pass and so may the people in it. It can be a depressing thought, especially if the person is someone who you really enjoyed being around, but it's helpful to understand that this is not necessarily a bad thing.

Chris came into my life exactly when God planned, in exactly the right season. He helped me gain the courage to move to a large city in order to attend WMU. He helped bring stability into my life. He gave me hope that there were nice guys out there who would love me for who I was, my dirty baggage and all. He didn't treat me second best to his buddies as past boyfriends had often done. I was first in his eyes. He didn't judge me for what my dad had done, he just tried to feel my pain even though he could not relate to it. He loved me and still loves me even though I am a natural worrier and perfectionist.

Just as we have to learn to appreciate the current season and whatever beauty it brings, so we have to grow to appreciate the people we have in our lives during any given time. We need to not fret over the people who were part of our stories at some point, but are no longer part of them now.

As we take time to reflect on the various people in our lives, we will begin to realize the purpose that each one serves, and the season that they helped us through. We also constantly have new seasons to look forward to and the relationships that they bring. Maybe someone new will come into our lives, or perhaps an old friend will return? My dad took his life in the spring but, although we didn't notice any outward signs, I think that he must have been struggling for quite some time. I believe that, in his mind, he left us many seasons prior to his death. For this reason, spring, with all its newness and growth, can still be a sad time for me. But with each year that passes, I realize that after spring I have summer to look forward to.

The word "season" not only refers to the time of year we find ourselves in, it can also be used as a verb. We add spice or flavor to food when we "season" it. This is such a great metaphor for the ways in which the people in our lives add color and flavor and spice to our stories. Our friends and family are the seasoning of our life's seasons! Without some of the people we have in our lives, I think we would all agree that things would be a little dull. I believe God knows exactly what we need in each season of our lives, be it winter, spring, summer or autumn. He also knows exactly which people will be right to help encourage, challenge and grow us during that season.

I once read an article about a man named Kevin Hines who jumped from the Golden Gate Bridge in September 2000. He was one of over 1700 people who have attempted suicide this way since the bridge was built in 1937. Only a known 25 have survived. While Kevin was on his way to the bridge to take his own life, he yearned for someone on the bus to just talk to him and show some concern. That didn't happen. After he jumped, he regretted it and prayed that he would survive while he was floating in the bay. He was rescued and entered a psychiatric facility to deal with his depression, paranoia and hallucinations. During his time in the facility, he met a priest who encouraged him to share his story. Kevin has helped many people since then.

There are many "if"s in life. If only a stranger had acknowledged Kevin and talked to him, he wouldn't have jumped. And yet, if he had not have jumped off the bridge and, as a result, met the priest, he wouldn't today be helping others who are struggling with suicidal thoughts of their own. I like to think that maybe Kevin was meant to go through his pain in order to allow him to meet the priest who encouraged him to help others.

Do you ever wonder why you meet the people you do? Do you wonder what their purpose is in your life or the purpose you have in theirs? I find myself wondering this every day when I meet new people. It's exciting when you finally figure out why you've met someone. I believe God places people in our lives for a reason. Unfortunately, sometimes it's easy to dismiss those people and miss an opportunity to learn something new about yourself or to help someone.

If you talk to and invite people into your life, you just may be able to help someone get through a hard season or you may even get ideas or advice for yourself about an issue you've been struggling with or a little project that will benefit you. The person you meet may have gone through the same struggle that you're currently dealing with and can help you get through it or vice versa. At times I'm thankful I blurted out my feelings, fears and struggles to someone who was just an acquaintance. Some acquaintances have become good friends and mentors to me over the years.

About ten years ago my mom went to her class reunion and started talking to someone whom she had had a crush on in middle school. They seemed to click and she contacted him a few weeks after the reunion. They have been companions ever since. She seems very happy with Jim. My siblings and I approve of him and admire how he respects my mom and helps her in any way that he can. They travel a little together, go out to dinner and spend time going to garage sales on weekends, or they just relax at her house while putting puzzles together. Jim has helped my mom during what could have been a very lonely season in her life.

I believe I met my friend Michele for a reason. Even though it started out badly, it has ended well. She has known me since we started kindergarten together, and although we had a tough middle/high school together, it worked out. We lost touch when I moved to Arizona but got back in contact with each other when I returned to Michigan. Whenever we get together, it's as if we start our conversation exactly where we left it last time. We often chat about our college years and laugh about the crazy things we've done. We also cry about having lost loved ones. Her dad overdosed when she wasn't yet a teen and her husband took his own life just over two years ago. Through seasons of grief, we've been able to stand by and support each other.

I met my friend Rebecca while living in Arizona. I designed a kitchen for her new home. She had worked with a few designers but liked my design the best. She became a special friend and was in the delivery room with Chris and me when our first daughter was born. She already had three kids of her own by this time so I knew she had more experience than we had! I figured she would know what to do to comfort me and prevent my husband from freaking out in the delivery room! She will hold a special spot in my heart forever. Since we moved back to Michigan, I haven't had a lot of contact with her but I know that God brought her into my life specifically for that reason during that particular season.

I think we all need at least one person who we feel safe with and who we know will be honest with us. Don't we all need a "Gayle" in our lives, just like Oprah Winfrey has? We need that one person who we could call in the middle of the night if we had to. After moving back to Michigan, I was envious of my friend Rebecca. She would talk about her close friend and her church family on the phone with me. One day, I asked her to pray for me that I would find a dear friend I could trust and confide in, someone who lived in my area. Rebecca prayed for me and I finally found that good friend. Her name is Deanna. I met Deanna through our daycare. Her son went to the same daycare as Reagan and then continued on to the same preschool. Deanna is sensible, honest, has good morals and is easy to talk to. She is someone I can vent to, trust and laugh with. She's the friend who helps me feel refreshed when I hang out with her. Her husband, Doug, is the same. He reminds me so much of my dad. He is a farmer and hard worker. His personality, although a little more outgoing than my dad, still reminds me of him in the way he likes to laugh, joke and have fun.

Soon after having children, I met Vicki who lives around the corner from us and who babysat my girls. Over the years, we have become close to Vicki and her husband. We, along with almost everyone else in the community, call them Nana and Papa. They are fun, honest, positive and generous people. They have been married for over 40 years and still act like newlyweds. They are a good role model for any married couple. We feel free to talk about our pasts with them and, knowing that they have also gone through many hardships together, we can get the advice we need to be able to make it through the difficult seasons. Vicki is a very spiritual person and often tells me to look for the signs that my dad is watching me and is with me. The stories she shares help me to not give up hope.

I think losing a loved one makes you want to believe that there is more to death than just the end of the road. It's common, after the death of a loved one, for people to become more spiritual and start searching for any signs that the loved one is still with them. I yearn for those special signs.

One day on my way to work, I was thinking about my dad while flipping through the radio stations. The song "The Old Rugged Cross" came on. I immediately got the chills. On another occasion, I was in church and started to think about my dad during worship time. The next song we sang was "The Old Rugged Cross." It was the only time I've ever sung that song while in church. My eyes began to tear up. I think about my dad often while at church. It's so easy to relate the pastor's sermons to what my dad might have been going through, feelings about hope, faith, struggle, love and many others. So many other people have helped and encouraged me in so many different ways. Christine and Howard directed me to God. Christine guided me to our church where I feel I have a church family who support me in what I do. Howard guided me to the Bible. He gave me an interest in learning about the Bible and making the Bible my "go to" with daily struggles. I will forever be thankful that, in part due to Howard, I know that I can trust in the Lord that everything will work out.

Meeting Debbie at church redirected my career path. It provided stability and contentment for me. It was exactly what I needed during that season of my life and especially with a second child on the way. Meeting Debbie also directed me to Jill who God used to answers my questions about my dad being in heaven. Thanks to my friendship with Jill I found my answer, literally in black and white.

Through Debbie, I was also able to meet Diana and help her in her struggles with celiac disease. Meeting Debbie not only helped me find the help I was needing in a particular season, but it also helped me to be the one to provide the support and encouragement needed by someone else in a particular season of their lives.

I have a friend, Kathleen, who is a colleague from the accounting firm that my husband and I both work at. Kathleen and I often discuss the books we've been reading and she recently suggested I read a book called, *Alla Lizzie* by Helen Eichstaedt. Once I started reading (and enjoying) it, I found out that my great aunt and uncle were in it. For years I have been wanting to put my story down on paper, but the thought of writing it down, and having enough to say, was overwhelming to me. Reading *Alla Lizzie* helped encourage me even more to write about my family. I learned more about my family's history reading that book. It also encouraged me to start looking up my ancestors. Ancestry can be fascinating! That little book gave me confidence in knowing that one doesn't need a 1000 pages to make a story complete.

My challenges and hesitations in writing continued when it came to what software program I should use to write this book. I was familiar with most of the Microsoft applications and knew that Excel could give me the ability to separate chapters, it wasn't practical to use for my purpose though. I also didn't want to invest in a new software program. One day, we had a training in our department meeting about OneNote. The more I listened to the speaker and learned what that program could do, the more I realized that this was exactly what I needed to use. It struck me then that, had I started writing before hearing more about the different software options available, I may have muddled my way along and potentially even given up in recording my story. I feel God has been creating a path and has been guiding me the entire way with this book which I'm so passionate about. As with the other seasons in my life, this season came at just the right time and provided the right opportunities to start recording my own narrative.

When my youngest daughter was in the first grade, her school held a breakfast to celebrate the mothers of elementary students around Mother's Day. I attended with hesitation. I knew that I wouldn't know a lot of people and I don't do well going to events without having a familiar face by my side. I ended up really enjoying the event. The speaker, Joy McMillan, spoke about how it takes a community to raise a child and what hard work it is to be a mother. It changed my life.

Joy, the owner of Simply Bloom, is a motivational speaker, writer, mentor and artist. Her book, *Penduka: 21 Ways To Awaken Passion & Purpose in Everyday Life*, gave me the motivation and encouragement to write and finish this book. It gave me hope that I could do something I am passionate about and step out of my comfort zone. We get so comfortable doing the same thing day after day, kind of like being on autopilot, we don't think about what we're doing, it just comes naturally. There have been many days where I arrive at work and can't recall how I've gotten there. I was either thinking about this book or everything that has to be done throughout that week. My "autopilot" must have kicked in.

Joy's book helped to ignite a passion in me. Writing my story down has excited me and left me feeling that I have a purpose while here on earth. Perhaps I can make a difference in someone's life? It also gave me the motivation to start my own decorating company again even if it's only part-time. I've realized that if you can do something you are passionate about, you will be a happier person. Being passionate about a particular job or hobby is a natural high that is very hard to explain. It is all you think about and all you want to do. It's as if you don't need any sleep because you don't want to stop doing what you love to take a break!

I know that I've met many other people, besides the ones mentioned here, who have had a positive effect on my life's journey. It's so easy to go through your day and not be aware of the impact someone may have just had on you. Some people just make you feel like a better person.

As we move through the seasons of our lives, some easier than others, it's so easy to get busy and forget to call or text a close friend. As you begin to appreciate the unique "seasoning" that each person might bring to your story, try to make time for your loved ones, close friends or even acquaintances. We may never know the difference that a simple "Hi" could make in the life of someone who is really struggling, but as we come to welcome and understand each season of our lives, and the value that each one has, we will grow to realize and be grateful for the many people God uses to add flavor to our histories.

"I know now that we never get over great losses;
We absorb them, and they carve us into
different often kinder, creatures.
You have to let people go.
Everyone who's in your life is meant to be
in your journey, but not all of them
are meant to stay till the end."
Gail Caldwell

CHAPTER 12
flourish

Flourish

fləriSH

> Noun 1. a bold or extravagant gesture or action,
> made especially to attract the attention of others.
> "with a flourish, she ushered them inside"
> 2. an impressive and successful act or period.
> Verb 1. to grow or develop in a healthy or vigorous way,
> especially as the result of a particularly favorable environment.
> Synonyms: grow, thrive, prosper, develop, increase,
> multiply "most plants seem to flourish in spring"

Twenty-five years have passed since my dad left this earth. It was, without question, the most defining event of my life. In many ways, I regret not writing this book earlier. It has been such a healing and therapeutic process for me. Although I could have started recording my story years ago, I believe that now was the time God intended for me to write this book, no sooner and no later. I have reached a stage of contentment and I no longer feel as overwhelmed as I once did.

I am so grateful for a loving husband, a good marriage, healthy children, a career I enjoy and the ability to start doing what I'm really passionate about. During the years of intense bullying, and then my father's suicide, growth seemed almost impossible. Instead of blossoming and flourishing, I retreated and faded. The parts of my character which had once given me such confidence made me doubt my abilities and question my faith. Years of personal struggle, career uncertainties and illness led to further anxiety and turmoil, so much so that, had I had an easy way out of my own life, I believe I may have taken it. And even when I realized that suicide just wasn't an option, the fight for progress in every area of my life seemed to be an unending one.

In order for a gardener to encourage the best growth from plants, the process of pruning is often necessary. Vital growth comes from cutting back branches, even those that sometimes don't seem like they need to be cut back. And although some of my life experiences can be likened to a pruning or cutting back by God in order to grow me more, others are those which I just rather would not have gone through. And yet I did. And I've made it to the other side. Growth has now come.

I may never know why God allowed those bullies in my life. I have questioned that since the bullying started. Maybe it was to make me become a stronger person, yet I don't think it achieved that. It only made me feel more timid and insecure. Maybe it was so I could experience the pain and help others who are dealing with the same issues. If the latter is true, then being bullied was worth the pain.

I have a deep desire to help those who are suffering as a result of bullying and also those who are desperate enough to be contemplating ending their lives. For these brave yet beaten souls, life seems unbearable. What they're going through seems more than just an opportunity to "toughen up and stick it out". I have always been concerned about family or friends or coworkers who may try to take their own life. Will I notice the signs? Will I get to them in time? Unfortunately, suicidal warning signs can go unnoticed even to a professional. I want to let my friends and acquaintances know of my story so they know there are other ways to deal with sadness. I wish the people who are contemplating suicide could look into the future and see the negative affect their suicide would have on so many people around them. Having been in the same situation, I understand how it would be so easy for people to make themselves believe that this world, their job, family, and friends would be better off without them. But they won't be. Suicide is a scar that will never completely heal. And yet the passage of time allows the scar to become less noticeable, less obvious and conspicuous.

I have a friend who I've only known a couple of years who attempted suicide approximately 20 years ago. As she told me her story, she said that she remembers it as if it were yesterday. By God's grace she survived the attempt and she now feels that time has helped to heal her wounds, although she knows the scars will always remain. As she looks back, she knows that she should have just gone to bed that evening, instead of dwelling on all that was going wrong in her life. The next day would have been a new fresh day. She has witnessed how much her suicide attempt has shattered her parents. The realization that her actions caused so much trauma has brought her immense pain.

I know that if through my story I could save just one person from suicide, many would actually be saved. A son or daughter, wife or husband, mom or dad would not have to go through the heartache that my family had to endure.

In looking back, and in the process of writing this book, I have discovered which habits, attitudes and practices have helped me to start flourishing. Above all, I've come to know that there is a God and that He hears me. Nothing is too small or too large to pray about. If it is important to you, it is important to God. And what may seem to be a small issue to one person, may not seem small to another person. Prayer has become a vital part of my day, a lifeline in the storms that have raged and will continue to rage.

I have learned that the ups and downs in life will come

and go. And there will be many more ups than downs. After finding the love of my life, getting married and having kids, I would not want my life to be any other way. I know that I have many more happy times to experience, such as the joy of seeing my girls grow up and witnessing their accomplishments in life, possibly their weddings and the births of my own grandchildren? I have the opportunity of doing what I love for the rest of my life and, God willing, growing old with my husband. There is so much still to look forward to.

At times, when life is going well and each day seems brighter than the previous, my pessimistic side gets the best of me. I wonder when something bad will happen. Will it be today, tomorrow or the next day? When life seems too good to be true, I start to worry. But suffering is normal. It does not matter if you are a Christian who goes to church every Sunday and prays daily, or if you have no religious background at all... bad things will happen. I was brought up to believe that only "true" Christians - those who pray, read the Bible daily and who go to church every week - do not have any hardships. However, this simply is not true. God never promised us an easy life, but He did promise to be with us when things are rough. I know that more pruning and cutting back may still happen in the days that lie ahead, but I've learned that I have no need to fear it, it's all part of the process.

> *"What we are is God's gift to us.*
> *What we become is our gift to God."*
> *Eleanor Powell*

God created each of us with a special gift. Figuring out

what that gift is, and taking time to pursue it, is key to finding our purpose in life. Having a purpose, I believe, is key to being able to turn the tide of suicidal thoughts around. Finding our niche in this world and discovering our God-given talents helps us to feel needed, valued, wanted or as though we're making a difference. Putting your heart and soul into something you love energizes you. I think I finally realized that my purpose is to decorate and to help others.

Whenever I can help someone else, I feel great about myself. I think that's why I also like design and decorating so much. I cannot make a difference in someone's life in other ways, but if I can help someone get their home in order so they feel more organized and put together, that makes me happy. Making homes and spaces beautiful fulfills me. I'm also uplifted by the people I form relationships with as I work on their homes. Some of these people have become great friends of mine and through many of their stories of trial and triumph, I've been able to learn so much. Knowing we're not alone in this journey of life can be such a comfort. As we reach out to others, we discover that all around us there are people going through painful situations. Simply recognizing that we're not the only ones experiencing the storms in life can open our eyes to the hope that lies ahead.

I've found that getting involved in my community and church has also enabled me to meet so many wonderful people. At times I felt I've been able to help one or two along the way, but many times it is I who have received the benefit of meeting and getting to know a new person. I think it's the little things that can make a difference in someone's life. Things such as saying "Hi" to a stranger or giving a coworker a cookie for no reason at all. These are the little moments that create connections between us and give us confidence. I believe that confidence is the key to realizing our worthiness. Many small, seemingly insignificant efforts go a long way to giving us confidence. From personal experience, I know that when I make an effort to dress nicely and put on some make-up, I immediately feel better about myself. The ripple effect of confidence, worth and purpose cannot be underestimated!

I've also learned the important role that journaling plays in helping to shape my thoughts. Writing down and recording my triumphs and tragedies, feelings and ideas, hopes and dreams has helped to put a voice to my experiences. Sometimes when one writes things out, they don't seem as bad as they did in your head! It's also a great way of keeping track of your progress, as you look back on days, weeks and years gone by. Being able to reflect on the direction one's life has taken is so key to staying on course.

I used to be constantly fearful that I would make a wrong decision or somehow take the wrong path in life. I now feel that God will gently guide and redirect us if we step off the path He intended for us. We need to continually ask and pray! One season in your life may appear dreary and may seem to never end or get better. It will though, and the next season may be so much better. While we have breath in our lungs, there will always be another chapter in our stories.

And with God as the ultimate author of our stories, it is up to us to pick up the pencil, turn the page and carry on writing. God has a plan for you.

As seasons of hardship and struggle have come and gone in my life, I am grateful for the opportunity to finally flourish. Age, wisdom, experience – all of these things have contributed to where I find myself now. As I think back to my childhood on the farm, and to my beloved lilac bush, I can see now what has enabled this season of thriving to finally come. It is the strong roots of family and faith, it is our branching out and reaching towards the light, it is living through the darkness and being able to stand up to the storm. Just like the hardiness that the lilac bush is known to represent, the ability to bloom despite the circumstances comes from being resilient and robust. Flourishing comes from experiencing the growth that is gained through the security of love and home, and in finding answers to those questions we all have. And finally, it is learning to live through and appreciate each season.

This is my story. I wouldn't have it any other way.

"I am a little pencil in God's hands. He does the thinking. He does the writing. He does everything and sometimes it is really hard because it is a broken pencil and He has to sharpen it a little more."

Mother Teresa

RESOURCES
help
WHILE YOU'RE IN THE STORM

Bullying information

Bullying is the use of force, threat, or coercion to abuse, intimidate, or aggressively dominate others. The behavior is often repeated and habitual. Bullying ranges from one-on-one, individual bullying or to group bullying called mobbing, in which the bully may have one or more "lieutenants" who may seem to be willing to assist the primary bully in his or her bullying activities. Bullying in school and the workplace is also referred to as peer abuse. Bullying can be physical, verbal, psychological or all three.

I believe that no child should ever feel alone or scared at school. Bullies will choose anyone as their victim. Also, there is a difference between being bullied and being teased. Bullying will occur day after day, consistently to the same person or people. Teasing is random.

According to the Stop Bullying Now Foundation:
- 60% of middle school students say that they have been bullied, while only 16% of staff believes that students are bullied.
- 160,000 students stay home from school every day due to bullying. (NEA)
- 30% of students who reported they had been bullied said they had at times brought weapons to school.
- A bully is 6 times more likely to be incarcerated by the age of 24.

- A bully is 5 times more likely to have a serious criminal record when he or she grows up.
- 2/3 of students who are targets become bullies.
- 20% of all children say they have been bullied.
- 20% of high school students say they have seriously considered suicide within the last 12 months.
- 25% of students say that teachers intervened in bullying incidents while 71% of teachers say they intervened.
- In schools where there are anti-bullying programs, bullying is reduced by 50%.
- Bullying was a factor in 2/3 of 37 school shootings reviewed by the US Secret Service.
- According to the National Institute of Occupational Safety Health (NIOSH) (Sauter, et al, 1990), there is a loss of employment amounting to $19 billion and a drop in productivity of $3 billion due to workplace bullying.

I feel empathy and sympathy when I hear of someone who is getting bullied.
- Bullying does not make you cool
- Bullying shows others that you are weak
- Bullying can leave permanent scars to sufferers

Unfortunately, bullying doesn't stop at teen years. Bullying can happen in a professional work environment but in different ways. People will do what they can, sometimes in a negative way, to get ahead in the workplace or get that promotion they feel they deserve. Some will stop at nothing and do not care if it includes bullying. Bullying can also happen in the home and with family members. This can either be emotional bullying or physical.

I believe bullying with young children starts in the home. Either the child sees it with his or her parents or is taught the behavior through their siblings. The child does not respect his or her parents so how could they ever respect their peers and treat them kindly?

I've contacted a couple of schools in my area asking about their protocol on bullying. I found out that the state law requires all Michigan schools to have an anti-bullying, which includes cyber-bullying, policy in place. This policy includes that all students "Are protected under the policy and that bullying is equally prohibited without regard to its subject matter or motivating animus." They also require that the schools report any incidents of bullying to the Department of Education on an annual basis. It is unknown what the department actually does with this information though. One local school uses the data as a part of their positive behavior intervention response system (PBIS). Hopefully this data will assist in stopping future bullying. In many surrounding schools, bullying assemblies either take place each year or every other year. I feel if schools continue to talk about bullying and make it a known issue and that it is frowned upon, maybe it will become less of an issue.

There are many ways to let an administrator know if bullying is taking place. One way is that students can tell any administrator themselves or send anonymous letters or emails via the district web site, the student can talk with a peer counselor who is usually a trained 11th or 12th grader in this matter, friends may come forward for their friends or administrators just may witness the bullying themselves. One school enforces the need for bystanders to step in when they witness bullying. If your peers stick up for you, the bully will react differently and back off. As with my case, it was two of us girls against almost my entire class. The bystanders need to display empathy, they need to stand up and not just stand aside. It will be scary and almost impossible for just one person so it takes a group. Even if you witness another student who is not your friend getting bullied. Stand up for him or her. It will make a difference.

Each bullying situation is unique and will be treated differently in each school with regards to the punishment. Once the administrator agrees that the case is a bullying case, and not just a little teasing, the bully will get a first warning. It may be that bully just felt a little mean or on edge that particular day and said or did something not nice to a certain person. If that same person is getting verbally or physically attacked on a daily basis, that is when the bullying is taking place. The administrator will talk this over with the victim and they will decide together what the next steps should be. Maybe it will be changing the victim's schedule so they aren't in the same classes as the bully or have to eat lunch during the same hour. Many times, unfortunately, once the bully is confronted, it makes matters worse for the victim. If this is a repetitive offense, the parents will get called. Michigan is a right to an education state and the most the bully could get suspended for is 45 days. However, each student has a right to be safe in their school too.

The administration has to show the victim positive behavior support. The victim has to believe that nothing is wrong with him or her, the bully is the person who has the issue. It's so easy though to think that you're the one who needs to change. In my case, I believe all of the bullies had underlying issues. They did not get the love and support from their family and felt the need to bully in school.

OK2SAY is the student safety program which allows students to confidentially report tips on potential harm or criminal activities directed at school students, school employees, and schools. It uses a comprehensive communication system to facilitate tip sharing among students, parents, school personnel, community mental health service programs, the Michigan Department of Health and Human Services, and law enforcement officials about harmful behaviors that threaten to disrupt the learning environment.

Helpful Resources to Prevent Bullying
- www.stopbullying.gov
- www.upstand.orgwww.thehumanityproject.com
- www.challengeday.org

Suicide Information:

In a 2016 report, the Centers for Disease Control found that about 84 out of every 100,000 people in the farming, fishing and forestry industries died by suicide in 2012. The suicide rate for the general population was about 12 out of every 100,000 people that year. That study included data from 17 states but did not include data from states like Iowa, Texas, or California where agriculture is a major part of the economy.

A study in 2017 done by researchers at the University of Iowa College of Public Health finds the suicide rate among farmers continues to be higher than other professions. From 1992 to 2010, there were 230 farmers who committed suicide across the United States.

A few of the triggers of farmers who commit suicide may be that they feel isolated, not having a lot of access to health care resources, which include mental health care resources. So if a farmer is suffering from depression, they may have less access to care for a mental health condition. Some of the issues, however, are directly related to the demands of the occupation. Farming can be stressful, mentally, physically and financially. It requires a lot of knowledge and faith that the weather will cooperate as it should for a successful planting and harvesting season. Unfortunately, when farmers see a therapist, most therapists don't understand what the farmer is going through. Quoted by one farmer, a therapist told him to take time off. "Unfortunately, cows will not milk themselves," was his reply.

According to ABC News on May 20, 2018, the Democrats turned down a farm bill that would have provided funding for crisis hotlines and other programs to provide mental health help to farmers. Per Republican Tom Emmer, "Our farmers who feed the world are feeling the weight of the world on their shoulders." The production cost of milk for small and medium dairy farmers is 10 to 30 percent lower than the price of milk.

The Farm Bill was originally created in 1933 as part of President Franklin D. Roosevelt's Agricultural Adjustment Act, which provided subsidies to U.S. farmers in the midst of the Great Depression. This bill not only helps farmers but ranchers and foresters also.

- It provides credit for beginning farmers to get started.
- It protects against farm and forest losses due to natural disasters through disaster assistance and crop insurance.
- It provides a cushion for the individual farmer if he or she suffers a poor yield or low prices, through a series of farm payment programs tied to specific commodities.
- It authorizes market access promotion and export credit guarantee programs that are key for promoting exports and generating farm income from exports.
- It provides a stable and secure supply of food for the nation. Along with efficient supply chains, they also allow us to enjoy relatively inexpensive food.
- The farm bill is also a nutrition bill. It funds the Supplemental Nutrition Assistance Program (SNAP), our country's major program that helps low-income individuals and families afford a healthy diet.
- Through the farm bill, Congress provides grants for research at land grant universities in fields ranging from

animal health to organic crop production and biotechnology.

For an interesting article on suicides within the farming community, please see the following link: https://www.cnn.com/2018/08/21/health/rural-suicides-among-farmers/index.html

Resources to Help Prevent Suicide & Educate People about Suicide:

- **National Suicide Prevention Lifeline** at 800-273-TALK (8255) or text "Go" to 741741
- **Question, Persuade, Refer:** https://qprinstitute.com
- www.suicidepreventionlifeline.org/
- www.suicideresourceandresponse.net/
- www.masponweb.org/index.htm
- www.suicidology.org/home
- www.jedfoundation.org/
- **American Foundation of Suicide Prevention:** https://afsp.org
- **Virtual Hope Box** (App for phone)
- **Suicide Prevention Resource Center's** self-paced online courses will help improve your knowledge and skills in suicide prevention. https://training.sprc.org
- **SafeTALK** is a half-day alertness training that prepares anyone over the age of 15, regardless of prior experience or training, to become a suicide-alert helper. www.livingworks.net
- **Applied Suicide Intervention Skills Training (ASIST)** is a two-day interactive workshop in suicide first aid for anyone over the age of 16. ASIST teaches participants to recognize when someone may have thoughts of suicide

and work with them to create a plan that will support their immediate safety.
- **Yellow Ribbon** is recognized as a best practice in suicide prevention and we a workshop is offered in both hour-long school assembly and 1.5-hour community presentation formats. In this workshop, Barb Smith Suicide Resource and Response Network staff will share stories to help identify others who may be at risk for suicide. Participants will be given the tools to help someone who may be depressed or suicidal as well as identifying community resources. www.yellowribbon.org
- **LivingWorks Education** is a suicide intervention training company that trains community helpers of all kinds to work in an intervention context. www.livingworks.net
- **The Walk for Hope… Depression and Suicide** Awareness is a 5k walk/run event held annually hosted by Barb Smith Suicide Resource and Response Network in Midland, Michigan. www.suicideresourceandresponse.net/event/walk-for-hope

ABOUT THE AUTHOR

Brenda Fitzmaurice was raised on a farm in a small town in Michigan and was brought up with good work ethics and the belief that family is important. She is happily married to her husband of 18 years and they have two adorable girls.
She loves spending time with her family, relaxing on the boat with her husband while he fishes, bike riding, reading and watching movies about real life events with her daughters.
She also loves shopping with her mom and friends.
Her passion has always been design and interior decorating, even as a child. She is the founder of Lilac Roots, LLC, where she is able to pursue her passion part time.
She also works in the finance department at a large accounting firm and continues to reside on 5 acres of pristine countryside in Merrill, Michigan.

NOTES

[1] *Psalm 55:1-9, 12, 13, New Living Translation (NLT)*
[2] *Psalm 55:15-19, NLT*
[3] *Barb Smith Suicide Resource and Response Network*
[4] *https://www.webmd.com/brain/news/20070829/bad-memories-easier-to-remember*
[5] *Isaiah 55:8-9, New International Version (NIV)*
[6] *https://www.cff.org/What-is-CF/About-Cystic-Fibrosis/*
[7] *To view this article online (under a slightly different title), please see:*
http://ronrolheiser.com/suicide-when-someone-is-too-bruised-to-be-touched
[8] *Romans 8:38, (NLT)*
[9] *Romans 3:23*
[10] *Matthew 11:28, NLT*
[11] *https://celiac.org/celiac-disease/understanding-celiac-disease-2/what-is-celiac-disease/*

Made in the USA
Lexington, KY
21 December 2018